celebratenewcomfortfoodseafoodwellnesscontemporaryglobalinspirationcelebratenewcomfortfoodseafoodwellnesscontemporaryglobalinspirationcelebratenewcomfortfoodseafoodwellnesscontemporaryglobalinspirationcelebratenewcomfortfoodseafoodwellnesscontemporaryglobalinspirationcelebratenewcomfortfoodseafoodwellnesscontemporaryglobalinspirationcelebratenewcomfortfoodseafoodwellnesscontemporaryglobalinspirationcelebratenewcomfortfoodseafoodwellnesscontemporaryglobalinspirationcelebratenewcomfortfoodseafoodwellnesscontemporaryglobalinspirationcelebratenewcomfortfoodseafoodwellnesscontemporaryglobalinspirationcelebratenewcomfortfoodseafoodwellnesscontemporaryglobalinspirationcelebratenewcomfortfoodseafoodwellnesscontemporaryglobalinspirationcelebratenewcomfortfoodseafoodwellnesscontemporaryglobalinspirationcelebratenewcomfortfoodseafoodwellnesscontemporaryglobalinspirationcelebratenewcomfortfoodseafoodwellnesscontemporaryglobalinspirationcelebratenewcomfortfoodseafoodwellnesscontemporaryglobalinspirationcelebratenewcomfortfoodseafoodwellnesscontemporaryglobalinspirationcelebratenewcomfortfoodseafoodwellnesscontemporaryglobalinspirationcelebratenewcomfortfoodseafoodwellnesscontemporaryglobalinspirationcelebratenewcomfortfoodseafoodwellnesscontemporaryglobalinspirationcelebratenewcomfortfoodseafoodwellnesscontemporaryglobalinspirationcelebratenewcomfortfoodseafoodwellnesscontemporaryglobalinspirationcelebratenewcomfortfoodseafoodwellnesscontemporaryglobalinspirationcelebratenewcomfortfoodseafoodwellnesscontemporaryglobalinspirationcelebratenewcomfortfoodseafoodwellnesscontemporaryglobalinspirationcelebratenewcomfortfoodseafoodwellnesscontemporaryglobalinspirationcelebratenewcomfortfoodseafoodwellnesscontemporaryglobalinspirationcelebratenewcomfortfoodseafoodwellnesscontemporaryglobalinspirationcelebratenewcomfortfoodseafoodwellnesscontemporaryglobalinspirationcelebratenewcomfortfoodseafoodwellnesscontemporaryglobalinspirationcelebratenewcomfortfoodseafoodwellnesscontemporaryglobalinspirationcelebratenewcomfortfoodseafoodwellnesscontemporaryglobalinspirationcelebratenewcomfortfoodseafoodwellnesscontemporaryglobalinspirationcelebratenewcomfortfoodseafoodwellnesscontemporaryglobalinspirationcelebratenewcomfortfoodseafoodwellnesscontemporaryglobalinspirationcelebratenewcomfortfoodseafoodwellnesscontemporaryglobalinspirationcelebratenewcomfortfoodseafoodwellnesscontemporaryglobalinspirationcelebratenewcomfortfoodseafoodwellnesscontemporaryglobalinspirationcelebratenewcomfortfoodseafoodwellnesscontemporaryglobalinspirationcelebratenewcomfortfoodseafoodwellnesscontemporaryglobalinspirationcelebratenewcomfortfoodseafoodwellnesscontemporary

Editor: Lydia Leong
Designer: Lock Hong Liang
Photographer: Aaron McLean

Published by Marshall Cavendish Cuisine
An imprint of Marshall Cavendish International
1 New Industrial Road, Singapore 536196

Other Marshall Cavendish Offices:
Marshall Cavendish Ltd.5th Floor, 32–38 Saffron Hill, London EC1N 8FH • Marshall
Cavendish Corporation. 99 White Plains Road, Tarrytown NY 10591-9001, USA •
Marshall Cavendish International (Thailand) Co Ltd. 253 Asoke, 12th Flr, Sukhumvit
21 Road, Klongtoey Nua, Wattana, Bangkok 10110, Thailand • Marshall Cavendish
(Malaysia) Sdn Bhd, Times Subang, Lot 46, Subang Hi-Tech Industrial Park, Batu Tiga,
40000 Shah Alam, Selangor Darul Ehsan, Malaysia

Marshall Cavendish is a trademark of Times Publishing Limited

National Library Board Singapore Cataloguing in Publication Data

Laris, David.
The menu / David Laris & Dean Brettschneider. – Singapore : Marshall Cavendish
Cuisine, c2009.
p. cm.
Includes index.
ISBN-13 : 978-981-261-623-4
ISBN-10 : 981-261-623-3

1. Cookery. 2. Baking. I. Brettschneider, Dean. II. Title.

TX714
641.5 -- dc22   OCN244258914

Printed in Singapore by Times Graphics Pte Ltd

Dedication

To Mum and Dad for your lessons, strength and passion for good food.

To my supportive wife, Trudi, who is the absolute love of my life, for enduring my bizarreness and the crazy schedule that is my life and for loving me back.

To Josephine, the sunshine in my life and my one and only daughter: the world got brighter the day you were born and I got softer.

~David Laris

To my loyal supporters and readers of my past four cookbooks. You are the reason why I continue to write more books. It's such a pleasure to receive so many encouraging emails and phone calls which makes it all worthwhile. You keep on reading and baking and I will keep on writing.

To Susan and my son Jason, the back bone of my career. It's hard to put in words how and what you have done to allow me to achieve and become who I am today. Thank you with all my love and thoughts. Susan, just keep on being you and Jason, follow your dreams, they do come true.

~ Dean Brettschneider

Contents

Acknowledgements

As with all books, there are so many people to thank, but top of our list is Aaron McLean, our photographer. We call him 'the magician' as he's such a pleasure to work with and knows how we think in terms of the style of photography that best represents our understanding of food and everything related to it.

Special thanks to Chris Newson, Violet Phoon, Lydia Leong and Lock Hong Liang at Marshall Cavendish International Asia for allowing David and myself to write and photograph the book with total confidence. As always it's great to work with a talented team of professionals.

Pantry Magic Pro Quality Kitchen Tools was there on hand to support us. They have an excellent range of professional and home cookware that we used throughout the book. We are grateful and look forward to our ongoing relationship.

Air New Zealand was there to help Aaron get to Shanghai and back to Auckland, allowing us to bring you the very best of cooking and baking through his camera lens. Thanks especially to Mike Tod and Ange Harold for their efforts in making it possible.

Thank you to the team at BakeMark China, in particular Jimmy Su, Sindy Huang, David Shen, Mark Chen, Tiffany Li and Li Williams for their support and encouragement throughout the photography session, and also allowing the use of the baking centre in Shanghai where the desserts, breads and pastries were made in the early hours of the morning before even David and Aaron were awake.

Thanks also to Shanghai-based photographer, Derryck Menere for his shots of David and myself at work.

~ DB

I would like to thank the teams at Laris Restaurant and David Laris Creates.

Jackie Xu for your tireless assistance in getting the ingredients list together, for being my memory when it failed me, and for taking the time to painstakingly check the quantities in the recipes, not to mention your strength of character and loyalty to great food and great kitchen teams. You are a pillar and an example to all.

Michelle Koh, I could not have finished this book without you. You are the structure that a person like me needs, for accepting the ridiculous deadlines given to tidy up the mess that was the first draft of this book and for doing it with a smile on your dial. Thank you for making it happen.

Jan Lu, for everything. For always being the best support a person could ask for and for the tireless updating of these pages while I was in the process of working on it, and of course for listening to all my impatient rants.

Jason Oakley, for your patience in putting up with me interrupting your operations with the process of making this book and for being such a talented chef.

Siobhan Gough, for your help in writing out the recipes and making sure the methods made sense.

The entire Laris teams for being just so damn good and the Slice Team for your super cool baking team.

Sandie Xu, Reto Kistler and Chris Wang for letting us run around the dining room with Aaron.

Diego Zhang, one of China's true natural wine palates, for the wine advice and the wine pairing. (Don't let the corporate world dull the passion.)

Vera Duerr for running around and just being a good sport about everything.

~ DL

Introduction

A word from David

When Dean first suggested we write a book of set menus for home cooks, I was hesitant, not because I have anything against family-style dining, but rather I had always imagined my first book would represent the body of work that I have created at my signature restaurant, Laris, a collection of fine dining menus that would be read by my fellow chefs. However, the more I thought about it, the more the idea made sense. After all, fine dining needn't be restricted to fine restaurants. And so with thanks to Dean, you now hold in your hands a book of great set menus, ranging from intimate meals for two, to large dinner parties, designed to bring the art of fine dining into your home.

Like most chefs, the kitchen is my home. And in that sense, Dean is an old friend of the family. He's given me some good advice over the years, but more importantly, he's demonstrated a passion for food that equals my own. When he comes to my restaurant, he sits down for a long leisurely meal. We rarely let him see a menu, we just cook for him.

The same sentiment applies to this book. Our aim is to encourage people who may normally not go through the trouble of preparing a set menu at home to do so. For those of you who already take the effort to do so, well, we hope to provide new inspiration. In these pages, we offer set menus that are well presented and easy to execute. We have tried to use ingredients that are quite readily available, with the odd surprise or two. We also include advice on wines and table service to compliment the menu. Whichever menu you first chose, we recommend that you make copies of it and place them on the table for your guests. By doing so, you will build anticipation for each dish, and prompt questions and debate, which will continue long after the meal has been consumed.

Over the years, I've participated in hundreds of cooking classes and demonstrations, and even appeared on the occasional TV show. To be honest, I like live demonstrations the most because that's where you get to see, feel and hear about people's passion for food. People like you; people who keep the idea of fine cooking at home alive and well, despite the ever-growing intrusion of over-processed, pre-packaged food into our lives.

Of course, those of you who love food, cook from scratch as often as you can, avoiding so-called convenience food like the plague. That said, finding fresh, natural ingredients isn't limited to shopping at your local health food store; if you don't believe me, check out the local markets. The availability of fresh produce will also have a co-relation with the average life span of that society.

Some of my earliest and fondest memories are of the fields in Greece, where my father grew acres of healthy

produce. Together we'd gather watermelons almost as big as I was then, as well as large red tomatoes, crisp lettuce, luscious ripe cucumbers and much more, to bring home to the family kitchen. But it was the olive harvesting season that left the most lasting impression on me. It was my job to help collect the olives off the ground, which I did rather reluctantly at first. But after experiencing the wonderful taste of the oil and cured olives they produced, I learned to appreciate the way things grow. In fact, I developed a profound respect for the land, and for the farmer. But more importantly, I learned the value of patience — to produce good food takes time. If you have ever cured your own olives, you will know what I mean.

Above all, have fun. If you attempt to produce a perfect meal for an important date, or for your superiors, bear in mind that things may not work out right the first time. If you insist on inviting VIPs to your first feast, try preparing the dishes several times before the big event. All the recipes included here work as single dishes, so feel free to play with them by substituting ingredients and even adapting them, if you're an experienced cook. Otherwise, follow the recipes for the best results.

Lastly, remember that love and passion are two of the most important ingredients in any menu. It is possible for two people to cook the same dish using the same ingredients, but with very different results. It could be that their techniques differed, but it's more likely they used unequal portions of love and passion. Keep those ingredients constant and after trying out the menus here, you can start swapping dishes amongst the various menus, keeping in mind not to repeat similar ingredients or textures in the starters and mains. Dean may not grant the same degree of freedom with his portion of the menu, but for good reason, as pastries and breads are a lot less flexible. But I'll leave it to him to tell you all about that.

May all your dinner parties be a great success.

A word from Dean

Entrenching baking further into the food world was foremost on my mind when I set out thinking about this book. I wanted to bring baking to the centre of the dining table, as I did with the four cookbooks I worked on earlier, in particular, *Global Baker*. I ended the book with a chapter about bringing desserts and petits fours formally to the dining table, and making them part of the meal experience. I call it "baking on a plate", since a complete dining experience would not exist if it were not for the humble baker, who is responsible for the breads at the start of the meal, to the dessert and finally the petit fours enjoyed as the final bow to a grand dining experience. So when preparing any of these menus, take the time to remember that baking is part of the food world, and make it part of your next dining experience.

I first met David in 2004 in Shanghai. I had not had the chance to dine at his signature restaurant, Laris then, but a friend told me that David insisted on baking his own bread there. That was music to my ears and it convinced me to make a visit. From the moment I walked in, I knew the experience was going to be among the very best I was ever going to have in fine dining restaurants around the world.

Having enjoyed a truly wonderful meal and dining experience, I met up with David for a chat and complimented him on the bread I was served. Always the perfectionist, I suggested that while he baked good bread, it could be better. That was the beginning of a great friendship.

I did not need to give a second thought to whom I wanted to collaborate with on this book, as David and I both share the same passion and vision, and most of all, we respect each other's part in bringing exceptional food to the table for others to enjoy.

My grandmother was a great home baker and the times we baked scones together provided an invaluable lesson on how important the feel of the dough is. "It's all in how you handle the dough" she would say. "Be gentle and don't mix it too much, otherwise you will toughen up the proteins in the flour and it won't rise." To this day, those words have stood me in good stead in my career as a baker.

Working with my hands came naturally to me and I was fortunate to be given the opportunity to become an apprentice baker, which was the start of my journey as baker and pastry chef. The learning curve was, and still is, very steep, but to me, a day not spent learning is a day wasted.

Born with a competitive nature, I needed no encouragement to forge ahead. Once I had made a clean sweep of the New Zealand baking competitions, I embarked on a career in the catering and hospitality industry in England, where I worked with some of the newly-crowned celebrity chefs in London's top and toughest pastry kitchens. This experience taught me much.

To me, baking is a 24-hour-a-day, seven-day-a-week, 365-day-a-year job. Passion is what drives me to achieve excellence in baking, but it's also my calling.

Today I'm based in one of the most exciting cities in the world, Shanghai. Baking in China has taught me many things. Patience, improvisation and the ability to communicate with just pointing and using hand gestures. There is a kind of international bakers' language, which I have had to use on more than one occasion. China has a well-developed baking culture, and I'm here to make a difference!

Sharing knowledge has always been a focus for my self development, which is one of the reasons why I wrote my first book on New Zealand baking. *The New Zealand Baker — Secrets and Recipes from the Professional* was the first comprehensive baking book written in New Zealand for home bakers. It was such a success that it won a Golden Ladle at the World Food Media Awards in 2001. This was a highlight in my career and one I will never forget. Imagine, my first book co-authored with Lauraine Jacobs, winning a major international award! We went on to write three more books together, winning another two international awards. *Global Baker* was launched in 2007 in New Zealand and 2008 across the globe. It will hopefully also gain international acclaim in years to come. These achievements have put baking at the centre of the table, along with food and wine, where it belongs. To me, baking is about passion, my uncompromising passion!

Happy baking!

about the
Recipes

The recipes, some classic and some that have been turned on their heads with respect to flavour combinations, textures, style and cultural eating habits, have been specially chosen to inspire the cook in you.

Some of you will gain inspiration from looking at the stunning photographs, while others will be attracted by the interesting recipes. But the most important thing is that you enjoy baking and cooking and getting your hands into the dough and batters, chopping and peeling those vegetables to prepare the perfect stock or going shopping to buy the best cut of meat and the freshest fillet of fish to make each recipe come to life.

Read through each recipe and menu carefully, a few times over, if need be, before you embark on preparing them, as some require advance preparation. Over and above all, one of the most important aspects of preparing a dinner party is having fun, so enjoy your experience and enjoy this book.

Setting the Scene

The scene you create is almost as important as the meal itself. You should always think this through and take the time to make it special. It will make all the difference.

It is important that when your guests arrive, they are immediately dazzled by the environment, lighting, music and set up, which all play a part in setting the mood. Have the canapés ready to go and the drinks chilled.

Something I love to do is to kick the evening off with a good strong conversation starter, such as a good stiff cocktail. There are many cocktails that have a nice punch without being unpleasant or too alcoholic in taste. Keep it to just one, however, before moving on to the champagne or wine. There is no point in getting your guests sloshed before they sit down to dinner, or they won't be able to appreciate all your hard work. You just want them to be relaxed, especially if they are new dining companions or perhaps family who may be overly judgmental.

Here are some things you must consider:

Tableware

Build up a collection of good quality cutlery and glassware. As the saying goes, "when an expensive glass breaks, it was simply its time". Glass lives, some longer than others, so what's the point of keeping your best items locked up? Enjoy them for as long as you have them. If you cannot afford expensive items, look for interesting individual pieces. It is all right if they are eclectic. They don't even have to match!

Glassware

Always polish you glassware. Do this is by holding the glass over a bowl of hot steaming water, then polishing with an absorbent cloth that does not leave behind fibres or streaks. Handle by the base only, or place the glass on the table using the cloth to hold the rim while polishing.

Cutlery

When polishing silver, start by washing well in super hot water, then polishing with a dry kitchen towel. You can also add a little vinegar to the rinsing water.

Plates

Take the time to select nice plates. As with the cutlery and glassware, they do not have to be expensive, but should be interesting. Squares, rectangles and rounds should all be part of your plate collection. Other must-haves are bowl plates, which are perfect for serving soups and pastas. Have them in different sizes, if possible, and try to stick to white or cream coloured ones. The food should be the star. Do not allow patterns to interfere with the presentation of your dish. A painter starts with a white canvas, not a floral one. You will notice that we have chosen to use white plates and repeat using the same plates several times over in this book. This is to show the effect of a good range that does not have to be all-encompassing, but just enough to create a design effect.

As with glassware, plates should always be polished. Wash in very hot water with plenty of soap, then rinse with hot water and allow to dry before polishing using a kitchen cloth. Alternatively, polish while wet. A good trick to clean off bits of sauce, or to remove fingerprints, is to use a cloth, dipped in a water and vinegar solution. The solution will evaporate leaving no streaks.

Tablecloth

I am a lover of crisp, white tablecloths. To me, there is no better canvas to begin to set your table on, than with a crisp, white tablecloth. This does not mean you cannot use other fabrics, or if you have a wonderful wooden table, it cannot simply be left bare. The point to bear in mind is that the tabletop should match your theme. If the setting is rustic, so should all the elements. It is also a nice touch if you use a coloured fabric to cover just the centre of the table. If you want to add contrast, try using a black tablecloth with white settings.

Placemats

If you are not using tablecloth, placemats are a good way to bring the table to life and define the settings.

Precision

It is very important that everything is placed in the correct position. You need to very pedantic about this. The glasses and cutlery should be spaced apart evenly, the flowers centred and so on. Take the time to step back from the table and review the layout one last time after you are done.

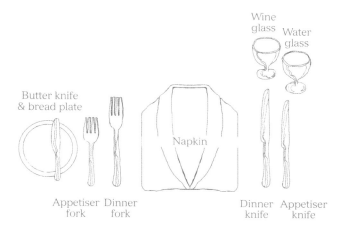

A suggested formal table setting

Wine

We have recommended wines to go with the food. You can also seek advice from a good wine shop, discussing with them the core elements of the dishes. Also check the correct temperatures to serve wines at. It is not as simple as reds not chilled and whites chilled. Some reds may need to be opened up earlier to allow them to breathe, so take the time to understand the wine you are serving. It is a big part of your dinner party experience.

Water

Do not neglect the fact that you should also serve water throughout the meal. Set water goblets and have a nice jug of water on the table or the side station, and be aware to top up the glasses throughout the meal. It is also a nice touch if you can offer bottled sparkling or still water. Take your pick of the many varieties available today.

Lighting

This is one of the most important elements which can be executed with candles. Use candles as a centrepiece or as part of a flower arrangement. Consider using a candelabra with lightly scented

candles. Bees wax candles are a wonderful touch. There are so many types and shapes. Take the time to shop for them. Tea light candles are lovely and can be used in abundance. It is also nice to place them in other parts of the room to create a soft setting. Use lamplight as well and avoid using the main room light, which may be too bright, unless you have a dimmer. The idea is to create mood and it is all right to have a variety of staged lighting throughout the house/apartment and the main dining room. The level of light should be comfortable and also reflect the occasion. For example, a business dinner would be more brightly lit than a romantic evening in.

Conversation

It is a good idea to have read the newspaper or flipped through a few magazines the day of the dinner party, so you can be current. Good conversation is one of the most important components of the evening. A good trick, if it is a dinner party with business associates or new friends, is to be aware of some of the interests of your guests. If the subject is new to you, read up enough about it to start a conversation, then let your guests show their knowledge. Most people love talking and showing their prowess on a subject. By setting this up, they will leave feeling good about themselves and your dinner party. Be equally ready to create conversation if the party goes quiet. With old friends and family, this may be less of a problem.

Music

This should be interesting and eclectic. Music should be there, but it should not be intrusive. Soft eclectic selections, such as a mixture of instrumental and vocal music, provide a good mix. The volume should be set at a level where it is there to be commented on if something interesting is being played but can disappear into the background if the conversation is running along nicely.

- **Brioche stuffing.** Start preparations a day ahead. Lay brioche cubes on a baking tray and leave uncovered to dry overnight.

- The following day, heat a pan and fry bacon until crispy, then add onion and butter. Cook until onion is soft and translucent. Add all remaining ingredients to pan. Mix well and remove from heat. Set mixture aside until cool enough to handle.

- On a clean work surface, lay out a sheet of plastic wrap about 25-cm (10-in) long. Place brioche mixture on plastic wrap in a long line, then roll up tightly into a cylindrical shape. Tie ends by twisting. Place roll in a steamer for 10 minutes, then remove. Set aside and allow to cool.

- Season turkey breast with salt and pepper, then brush with some butter. Roast in a preheated oven set at 180°C (350°F) for 20 minutes.

- While turkey is roasting, heat a pan and stir-fry French beans until tender. Unwrap brioche stuffing, cut into 8 equal slices, then sear on both sides until golden. Keep stuffing warm in the oven. Heat giblet gravy in a pot.

- Place 3–4 French beans on each plate. Top with one slice of stuffing, then turkey breast and finish with more French beans. Pour cranberry sauce and giblet gravy over, and spoon some more sauce on the side of each plate. Place another slice of stuffing on each plate.

sour cherry & cranberry trifle *serves 4*

What would Christmas be without a trifle? This one features cranberry jelly, cherries, custard and cream, so there is plenty of sharpness combined with a creamy sweetness.

Basic sponge (page 203)	1 quantity, cut it into 1-cm (¹/₂-in) cubes, or use store-bought sponge fingers and store excess in the freezer until needed
Crème chantilly (page 204)	1 quantity
Fresh strawberries	4
Chocolate sticks	8

Cranberry jelly

Gelatine leaves	2 sheets
Cranberry juice	300 ml (10 fl oz / 1¹/₄ cups)
Sugar	50 g (1²/₃ oz)

Custard

Milk	250 ml (8 fl oz / 1 cup)
Single (light) cream	75 ml (2¹/₂ fl oz)
Vanilla pod	1, split and seeds scraped
Eggs yolks	2
Sugar	15 g (¹/₂ oz)
Corn flour (cornstarch)	1 tsp

Sour cherry filling

Corn flour (cornstarch)	1 Tbsp
Canned sour cherries (stoned)	1 can, 425 g (15 oz)
Vanilla pod	1, split and seeds scrapped

- **Cranberry jelly.** Soak gelatine leaves in a bowl of cold water. Squeeze out excess water before use. In a small saucepan, heat cranberry juice and sugar until just about to boil. Remove from heat, add softened gelatine leaves and stir to dissolve. Set aside to cool, then pour into a jug. Use while still liquid.

- **Custard.** In a saucepan, bring milk, cream and vanilla pod and seeds to simmering point slowly over low heat. Remove vanilla pod. (The pod can be washed, dried and placed in a jar with castor sugar to make vanilla sugar.)

- In a separate bowl, whisk egg yolks, sugar and corn flour together until well blended. Pour hot milk and cream over eggs and sugar, whisking all the time. Return mixture to the saucepan and stir gently with a wooden spatula over low heat until thickened. Pour custard into a jug and cover with plastic wrap. Leave to cool a little. Use while still of pouring consistency.

- **Sour cherry filling.** Strain canned sour cherry juice into a bowl. Place cherries in a separate bowl and set aside. Measure out 150 ml (5 fl oz) cherry juice and place in a small saucepan with vanilla pod and seeds. Bring to the boil.

- Mix corn flour with 1 Tbsp cherry juice to make a slurry. When cherry juice comes to the boil, remove from heat and whisk in cherry slurry. Return to medium heat for 2 minutes to thicken, stirring all the time. Remove from heat and stir in strained cherries. It is okay if a few cherries break up while stirring, as this will create texture in the filling. Pour filling into a bowl and cover with plastic wrap. Leave to cool until required.

- **To assemble.** Use four 250-ml (8-fl oz / 1-cup) glasses. Lean glasses at an angle and place 5–6 sponge cubes at the bottom of each glass. Pour in cooled liquid cranberry jelly, then refrigerate, still at an angle, until jelly sets. Stand glasses upright and pour some custard in. Spoon in some cherry filling, then fill with some crème chantilly, levelling off the top. Decorate with fresh strawberries and chocolate sticks.

chocolate fruit &
nut drops *makes about 50*

These little chocolates are full of fruit and nuts and are great as a finishing touch to your dinner. They are simple to make, but choose the fruit and nuts carefully, so the final product will be impeccable.

Quality dark, milk or white chocolate	250 g (9 oz)
Pistachio nuts or small whole almonds or hazelnuts	50
Dried cranberries	50
Dried apricots	10, cut into strips

- Chop chocolate into pieces, then place in a bowl set over a saucepan of simmering water. Stir until chocolate is melted.

- Line a baking tray with non-stick baking paper. Spoon small circular teaspoonfuls of melted chocolate on tray. Do only 10 at a time or chocolate discs will harden before you are able to complete garnishing them.

- When chocolate is just starting to set, place a nut, a dried cranberry and a piece of sliced apricot onto each disc. Allow chocolate to fully set before removing from baking paper.

poached mandarin fish & kai lan with chinese rice noodles *serves 4*

Steaming is the perfect way to enjoy the full flavour of fish.

Mandarin fish fillets with skin	4 fillets
Chinese rice noodles	200 g (7 oz)
Kai lan	8 stalks, blanched
Ginger	50 g (1²/₃ oz), peeled and julienne
Leek	50 g (1²/₃ oz), white part only, julienne
Long red chilli	1, deseeded and julienne
Coriander leaves (cilantro)	5 g (¹/₆ oz)
Vegetable oil	4 tsp

Soy broth

Vegetable oil	50 ml (1²/₃ fl oz)
Celery	¹/₄ stalk, diced
Leek	¹/₄ stalk, diced
Carrot	¹/₄, diced
Coriander leaves (cilantro)	a small bunch, chopped
Chives	a small bunch, chopped
Garlic	3 cloves, peeled and chopped
Ginger	1 thumb-size knob, peeled and chopped
Star anise	1
Cinnamon stick	1
Dark soy sauce	5 tsp
Light soy sauce	5 tsp
Hua tiao wine	50 ml (1²/₃ fl oz)
Thick dark soy sauce	5 tsp
Thai fish sauce	1¹/₂ tsp
Chicken stock (page 205)	500 ml (8 fl oz / 2 cups)

- **Soy broth.** Heat oil in a pan and sweat diced vegetables until soft. Add all other ingredients and bring to the boil. Reduce heat and simmer for 1 hour. Pass mixture through a fine sieve and set aside.

- Steam fish for 10 minutes in a bamboo steamer.

- Meanwhile bring some water to the boil in a large saucepan. Add noodles and some cold water. Allow water to return to the boil, then strain noodles and set aside.

- Arrange kai lan on serving plates. Take a small handful of noodles and wrap it around a fork to create a tight ball. Arrange noodles on the side of vegetables. Reheat soy broth and pour over vegetables.

- **To serve.** Place steamed fish, skin side up on top of noodles and vegetables. Garnish with julienne ginger, leek, chilli and coriander. Heat vegetable oil and spoon over fish.

This crème brûlée has a rough texture compared to the classic version because of the sweet potato purée. Chinese wolfberries are high in antioxidants. They are beneficial to the immune system and liver, and contribute to eye and heart health.

sweet potato *&* chinese wolfberry crème brûlée with lavender tuile springs *serves 4*

Sweet potato crème brûlée

Chinese wolfberries	100
Sweet potatoes	2, large, scrubbed clean
Eggs	2
Egg yolks	4
Sugar	120 g (4$^1/_2$ oz)
Castor (superfine) sugar	400 g (14$^1/_3$ oz)
Double (heavy) cream	500 ml (16 fl oz / 2 cups)

Sweet potato purée

Sweet potatoes	2, large, scrubbed clean
Boiling water	50 ml (1$^2/_3$ fl oz)
Icing (confectioner's) sugar	50 g (1$^2/_3$ oz)

Lavender tuile springs

Tuile paste (page 211)
Lavender flowers

- **Sweet potato crème brûlée.** Soak Chinese wolfberries in warm water for 1 hour to plumb them up. Drain before using.

- Using a microwave oven, cook sweet potatoes in their skin until soft. Takes about 5 minutes on High. Leave to cool slightly, then cut and dig out flesh. Purée with a hand-held blender, then press purée through a fine sieve. Measure out 150 g (5⅓ oz) purée.

- In a small bowl, whisk sweet potato purée, eggs, egg yolks and half the sugar together.

- In a saucepan, bring cream to the boil, then remove from heat and whisk into egg mixture. Strain and pass custard through a fine sieve into a pouring jug.

- **Sweet potato purée.** Using a microwave oven, cook sweet potatoes in their skin until soft. Leave to cool slightly, then cut and dig out flesh. Purée with a hand-held blender, then press purée through a sieve.

- Mix boiling water with icing sugar and add to purée. Mix until smooth. Place into a small bowl and cover with plastic wrap. Refrigerate to firm up.

- **Lavender tuile springs.** Make a long strip stencil 15–20 cm (6–8 in) long and 1 cm (½-in) wide. Spread tuile paste over stencil on a baking tray lined with non-stick baking paper. Remove stencil and make another 2 tuiles. Sprinkle some lavender flowers evenly over tuiles.

- Place tray in the oven and bake until tuiles are light amber in colour. While tuiles are still warm, wind each one loosely around a wooden spoon handle. Work quickly, one at a time. Should baked tuiles harden flat on the tray, reheat tray to soften tuiles.

- **To finish.** Place 4 ovenproof bowls into a roasting pan, then half-fill pan with water. Place about 25 soaked and drained wolfberries into each bowl, then pour brûlée mixture over until almost to the brim. Carefully transfer roasting pan to preheated oven set at 150°C (300°F) and bake for 25–30 minutes, or until brûlée is set, taking care not to spill water or brûlée mixtures.

- Carefully remove pan from oven. Place bowls of brûlée into the refrigerator to cool.

- Just before serving, remove bowls of brûlée from the refrigerator and sprinkle tops evenly with remaining sugar. Caramelise sugar using a blowtorch or under a hot grill.

- Using 2 tablespoons, make quenelles from chilled sweet potato purée and place on top of brûlée. Sit a tuile spring over.

petite red bean madeleines

makes 24

Red bean paste is common throughout Asia and can be bought ready made from Asian specialty food shops. The store-bought version is typically smoother. Red bean paste is often used as a filling for steamed buns, Chinese pancakes and mooncakes. Combining the Asian paste with the French Madeleine presents a wonderful and unusual taste experience.

Sweet red bean paste filling

Dried red beans	55 g (2 oz)
Sugar	1/4 cup
Vegetable oil	2 Tbsp

Batter

Plain (all-purpose) flour	125 g (4 1/2 oz) + more for dusting
Baking powder	1/2 tsp
Salt	a pinch
Butter	60 g (2 oz), melted + more for greasing Madeleine mould
Egg	1
Castor (superfine) sugar	100 g (3 1/2 oz)
Warm milk	8 tsp

- **Sweet red bean paste filling.** Start preparations a day ahead. Wash beans and discard any with blemishes. Place in small saucepan, cover with water and leave to soak overnight. The following day, bring beans and water to the boil. Simmer for 1 1/2–2 hours, until beans are soft. Add more water as necessary. Remove from heat and drain. Place beans in a blender and purée until smooth. Add sugar and blend again.

- Heat oil in a frying pan. Add bean paste and cook over medium-low heat, pressing paste against pan with the back of a spatula or wooden spoon to form a cohesive paste. This will take a few minutes. Cool and use, or store refrigerated for up to 2 weeks.

- Lightly grease a petite Madeleine mould with melted butter and coat with flour, tapping off any excess flour.

- **Batter.** Sift flour, baking powder and salt into a bowl.

- Place egg and sugar into the mixing bowl of an electric mixer fitted with a whisk attachment. Whisk until thick and creamy. The process may be quickened by placing the mixing bowl over a saucepan of warm water while whisking from time to time.

- Slowly add milk and 50 g (1 2/3 oz) red bean paste to mixture while still mixing on slow speed. Gently fold in sifted dry ingredients, taking care not to over mix and knock all the air out of the mixture. When dry ingredients are three-quarters way mixed in, gently fold in melted butter to get a creamy supple paste.

- Scoop about 1 tsp batter into each pre-greased and floured Madeleine mould. Place directly into a preheated oven set at 210°C (410°F) and bake for about 5 minutes, or until each Madeleine springs back when lightly touched. The amount of filling and baking times will vary depending on the size of the Madeleine mould.

- Remove Madeleines from mould immediately and leave to cool on a wire rack. Quickly cool mould to use again for next batch of Madeleines.

valentine's

Chocolate, Pecan & Cranberry Sourdough

Trio of Oysters
Red Wine Vinegar & Shallot Foam
Fresh Wasabi & Flying Fish Roe
Peppergrass Cress & Lime Salsa
Wine: Chardonnay, Chablis

★★★

**Beef Tenderloin with Pancetta, Foie Gras Terrine,
Porcini Mushrooms & French Beans**
Wine: Bordeaux Blend (less tannin)

**Raspberry Macaron Tart with Raspberry Cream,
Blueberry Compote & Red Currants**
Wine: Moscato d'Asti or Sweet Sparkling Red Wine, Italy

**Heart Jam Dodgers
Strawberries & Cream Truffles**

Tea & Coffee

chocolate, pecan *&* cranberry sourdough *makes 2 loaves*

This is one of my favourite bread recipes. Don't expect this loaf to be light and fluffy in texture, as the excessive amount of fruit, nuts and chocolate makes it a dense and compact loaf. Slice and serve with butter and enjoy with a sweet Riesling.

Bread flour	350 g (12 oz)
Basic levain or sourdough starter (page 200)	180 g (6½ oz)
Cocoa powder	20 g (⅔ oz)
Water	230 ml (7¾ fl oz)
Salt	1¼ tsp
Dried cranberries	80 g (2⅘ oz)
Chopped pecans	80 g (2⅘ oz)
Broken chocolate pieces or chocolate chips	80 g (2⅘ oz), refrigerated overnight

- In a large mixing bowl, combine flour, starter, cocoa and water with a wooden spoon into dough. Tip dough out onto a lightly floured work surface and knead for 10–15 minutes, taking a rest of 30 seconds every 3–4 minutes, until dough feels smooth and elastic. Place dough into a lightly oiled bowl and cover with plastic wrap. Leave to rest for 20 minutes in a warm place.

- Tip dough out onto a lightly floured work surface, then add salt and knead until salt is fully incorporated and dough is smooth and elastic. Takes 3–4 minutes. Add cranberries, pecans and chocolate, and knead until evenly combined with dough. Place dough into a lightly oiled bowl and cover with plastic wrap. Leave in a warm place until almost doubled in size. Takes about 3 hours.

- Tip dough out onto a lightly floured work surface and gently deflate it by folding it onto itself 3–4 times. Return dough to lightly oiled bowl and cover with plastic wrap. Leave for another hour in a warm place.

- Meanwhile, line 2 cane proofing baskets or 2 medium round bowls with clean tea towels, then dust lightly with flour.

- Tip dough out onto a lightly floured work surface and halve. Gently mould each piece into a ball by cupping your hands around it and moving in a circular motion, pulling the skin tight over the dough. Don't overdo it, or the skin will rip and spoil the appearance of the final product. The dough will be smooth with a rough, scrunched-up bottom.

- Place loaves seam side up in the floured cane proofing baskets or medium round bowls lined with a tea towel. Allow to rise in a warm place for about 2 hours, or until dough is almost doubled in size. Cover with plastic wrap to prevent skinning and chilling of the dough.

- Preheat oven to 240°C–250°C (465°F–475°F), with a baking stone or heavy baking sheet in place. Gently tip loaf out onto a peel lightly dusted with semolina or polenta. Using a razor blade or sharp knife, cut a trellis pattern on the top of each loaf. Just before placing in oven, spray water into oven cavity with a spray gun.

- With the peel and loaf in one hand, open the oven with the other, and gently "flick" the loaf off the peel and onto the baking stone or sheet. Close oven door immediately and leave for 2 minutes, then repeat to "steam" oven again. Resist opening the oven door for another 20 minutes. After the first 20 minutes, turn the heat down to 200°C (400°F), and check loaf for even baking. After 30–35 minutes, the loaves will be ready. Remove and cool on a wire rack.

- **To serve.** Cut sourdough into slices and serve with lightly salted butter.

petite garlic & coriander naan *makes 15*

Naan is a popular Indian flat bread. Here, I have added garlic and coriander to give it an extra kick of flavour. Naan is best served hot, straight from the oven, freshly brushed with melted butter.

Strong bread flour	280 g (10 oz)
Plain yoghurt	60 g (2 oz)
Salt	5 g (1/6 oz)
Honey	2 tsp
Garlic	1 clove, peeled and finely chopped
Butter	15 g (1/2 oz), melted + more for brushing bread
Ground coriander	1 tsp
Active dried yeast	5 g (1/6 oz)
Water	125 ml (4 fl oz / 1/2 cup)
Black onion seeds or nigella seeds	2 tsp
Finely chopped coriander leaves (cilantro)	1 1/2 Tbsp

- In a large mixing bowl, place flour, yoghurt, salt, honey, garlic, melted butter, ground coriander, yeast and water. Mix together to form a firm dough. Tip dough out onto a lightly floured work surface and knead for 10–15 minutes, taking a rest of 30 seconds every 3–4 minutes, until dough feels smooth and elastic.

- Add black onion seeds or nigella seeds and chopped coriander during the last 2 minutes of mixing. Knead until well incorporated. Place dough into a lightly oiled bowl, cover with plastic wrap and leave in a warm place until almost doubled in size. Takes 30–45 minutes.

- Tip dough out onto a lightly floured work surface and divide into 15 equal pieces. Mould each piece into a ball and cover with plastic wrap. Leave for another 30 minutes in a warm place.

- Using a rolling pin, roll each ball out on a floured work surface into a teardrop shape about 0.5-cm (1/4-in) thick. Place on a well floured work surface and cover with plastic wrap for another 15–20 minutes to rise.

- Preheat oven to 250°C (475°F) and place an oven tray into the middle shelf of oven. If you have a pizza stone, place it in the oven 1 hour before baking to ensure it is well heated.

- Bake naan in batches of 2 or 3. Gently place naan onto a cool baking tray lined with baking paper. Open oven door and slide baking paper with naan directly onto preheated oven tray or pizza stone. Bake for 3–4 minutes, until naan is puffed up and brown in spots.

- Remove baked naans from oven and brush with melted butter while still hot, so naan will be soft and have a buttery flavour. Repeat with each batch of naan.

- **To serve.** Brush naan with melted butter and serve hot. Naan can be made ahead of time and reheated in a hot oven just before serving.

layered carpaccio of beef pecorino *serves 4*

Beef tenderloin	280 g (10 oz), covered with plastic wrap and placed in the freezer for at least 3 hours
Aioli (page 204)	4 tsp
Chervil	
Chives	

Pecorino-caper-anchovy paste

Canned anchovies	28 g (1 oz)
Shallots	2, small, peeled and chopped
Pecorino cheese	180 g (6½ oz), finely grated
Capers	48 g (1½ oz), chopped
Basil	4–5 leaves, chopped
Parsley	a handful, chopped
Lemon juice	2 tsp
Virgin olive oil	7 tsp
Ground black pepper	½ tsp

Chive oil

Olive oil	2 tsp
Chives	30 g (1 oz)

Traditionally, this dish is served with the thinly sliced meat laid flat and the ingredients sprinkled over the top. The twist here is that the ingredients are made into a paste. This allows you to get away with not having a slicing machine, as the meat can be beaten to flatten it, since the need for perfect slices is less important.

- **Pecorino-caper-anchovy paste.** Finely chop anchovies until pasty, then place in a bowl with shallots, cheese, capers, basil and parsley. Mix well, then add lemon juice and blend in olive oil. Season with pepper.

- **Chive oil.** Blend oil with chives. Strain through a chinoise.

- **To assemble.** Unwrap frozen beef and slice it as thinly as possible with a sharp knife so that beef is almost transparent. Alternatively, ask your butcher to do this. Using a cutting ring about 6-cm (2½-in) in diameter, cut discs out from sliced beef.

- Still using the cutting ring, layer beef and anchovy paste alternately in 4 equal height stacks. The layers of beef and anchovy paste should be equally thin. Over time and with more practise, you will achieve a neat stack, although the taste of the dish will not be affected even if the stack is not perfect. The key objective is to make the stacks about the same height, with a smooth finish on top. The top layer should be beef. Spread a little aioli over the top beef layer and smoothen it out. With a palette knife or butter knife, gently lift carpaccio stack onto a serving plate and slip the cutting ring off. Repeat to make another 3 stacks.

- Dot plate around carpaccio stack with chive oil using the end of a knife or a tear dropper. Garnish with chervil and a chive tip. If you are feeling ambitious, garnish with grissini (page 67).

risotto of porcini mushroom, chicken breast & mascarpone with crispy skin & lemon foam

serves 4

Risotto is truly one of life's good things. The magic here is the addition of mascarpone, which gives the dish a creamy texture that your guests will remember for a long time. Bear in mind that risotto is a slow-cooked dish that requires a lot of love in its preparation.

Risotto

Butter	100 g (3$^1\!/_2$ oz), cubed + more for cooking mushrooms, onion and garlic
Porcini mushrooms	200 g (7 oz), sliced
Salt	to taste
Ground black pepper	to taste
White onion	150 g (5$^1\!/_3$ oz), peeled and chopped
Garlic	10 g ($^1\!/_3$ oz), peeled and chopped
Arborio rice	500 g (1 lb 1$^1\!/_2$ oz)
White wine	250 ml (8 fl oz / 1 cup)
Chicken stock (page 205)	500 ml (16 fl oz / 2 cups) + 100 ml (3$^1\!/_3$ fl oz)
Mascarpone cheese	80 g (2$^4\!/_5$ oz)
Parmesan cheese	160 g (5$^2\!/_3$ oz), grated
Lemon	1, juice extracted

Chicken breast & skin

Free-range chicken breasts with skin	4
Milk	800 ml (27 fl oz)
Sour cream	20 g ($^2\!/_3$ oz)
Salt	to taste
Ground black pepper	to taste

Garnish

Lemon foam (page 206)	as needed
Arugula (rocket) leaves	

- **Risotto.** Heat a small knob of butter in a pan and sauté mushrooms lightly. Adjust taste with salt and pepper. Set aside.

- Heat some butter in a pan and sweat onion and garlic over low heat until soft. Add rice, stirring continuously to coat all grains with butter. Deglaze with white wine, then gradually add chicken stock, stirring continuously. Note that rice should not be absorbing stock too quickly. Continue to simmer over low heat until rice is cooked al dente. Finish by stirring in cubed butter and cheeses. Adjust seasoning with salt and pepper and add lemon juice.

- **Chicken breast & skin.** Clean chicken breasts, then remove and reserve skins. Marinate chicken breasts with milk, sour cream and seasoning, then place each breast into individual zipper storage bags and seal. Place into a pot of simmering water and poach slowly over low heat for 25–30 minutes.

- Clean skin and take off fat. Line a baking tray with baking paper and lay chicken skins out flat. Season with salt and pepper, then place another sheet of baking paper directly on top of skins. Weigh down with another baking tray to keep skins flat while baking. Bake in a preheated oven set at 170°C (330°F) for 20 minutes.

- **To serve.** Spoon mushroom risotto onto serving plates. Slice chicken breasts and arrange over risotto. Top with lemon foam and crispy chicken skin. Garnish with arugula.

An interesting combination of chocolate and blue cheese makes this dessert unique. The sweetness of the praline and caramel sauce balances well with the blue cheese. If you don't like the idea of blue cheese, replace it with fresh or frozen raspberries.

chocolate & blue cheese tortellini with vanilla ice cream, crunchy praline & caramel sauce *serves 4*

Vanilla ice cream
  (page 211)

Tortellini

Cocoa powder	15 g (1/2 oz)
Hot water	2 Tbsp
Melted dark chocolate	2 Tbsp
Eggs	2
Plain (all-purpose) flour	200 g (7 oz)
Sugar	50 g (1²/₃ oz)
Egg wash	made by lightly beating 1 egg with 3 Tbsp water

Filling

Double (heavy) cream	75 ml (2¹/₂ fl oz)
Dark chocolate	150 g (5¹/₃ oz), chopped into small pieces
Unsalted butter	1 Tbsp
Blue cheese	100 g (3¹/₂ oz)

Crunchy praline

Sugar	100 g (3¹/₂ oz)
Lemon	1, cut in half
Almond flakes	100 g (3¹/₂ oz), lightly toasted

Caramel sauce

Water	50 ml (1²/₃ fl oz)
Sugar	60 g (2 oz)
Double (heavy) cream	150 ml (5 fl oz)

- **Filling.** Place cream in a microwave-safe bowl and heat in the microwave oven on High until just about to boil. Stir in chocolate and butter until melted and combined. Cover and leave to cool for 2 hours until firm. Blue cheese is used only when making up tortellini.

- **Tortellini.** In a small bowl, mix cocoa with hot water into a paste. Place cocoa paste, melted chocolate, eggs, flour and sugar into a mixing bowl and bring together until dough is formed. Knead by hand until dough is smooth and elastic. Takes about 10 minutes with short rests in between to make kneading easier. Add a little flour if dough feels too sticky.

- Cover dough with plastic wrap and refrigerate for 1 hour to firm up a little. Roll out chilled dough on a lightly floured work surface into a rectangular sheet about 0.3-cm ($^1/_8$-in) thick, then cut into 12 squares, each about 7.5 cm (3 in).

- Place about 1 tsp chocolate filling in the centre of each square and top with $^1/_2$ tsp blue cheese. Brush edges of dough with egg wash, fold over the square to form a triangle, then pinch edges to seal. Pull the 2 far ends of triangle together and pinch firmly to make tortellini. Repeat with rest of ingredients.

- Tortellini can be made ahead of time, then kept covered in the refrigerator.

- **Crunchy praline.** Place sugar in a clean, dry pan over low heat and stir continuously with a clean, dry spoon until light golden in colour. Add a squeeze of lemon juice, then toasted almond flakes and tip mixture immediately onto a lightly oiled work surface. Leave to cool, then crush into small pieces with a rolling pin. Store praline in an airtight container.

- **Caramel sauce.** Boil water with sugar in a small pan until golden in colour. Remove from heat and stir in cream. Return to heat and simmer for a few minutes.

- **To serve.** Cook tortellini in simmering water until they float. Takes about 3 minutes. Drain and keep warm.

- Place a small amount of crunchy praline in the middle of a serving plate and top with a scoop of vanilla ice cream. Arrange 3 tortellini around ice cream on each plate, then drizzle some caramel sauce around. Serve immediately while tortellini is still warm.

fruit marshmallow cubes on a sesame seed brandy snap puddle

makes about 100 marshmallows

Marshmallows are old-fashioned, but at the same time, very retro. This recipe yields melt-in-your-mouth marshmallows, unlike the rubbery, chewy commercial ones from supermarkets. Use lots of different flavours and colours to inject some fun into the end of the evening. The brandy snap puddle is a fun way to serve these petit fours, and it can be eaten too!

Marshmallows

Gelatine powder	20 g (^{2}/$_3$ oz)
Cold water	180 ml (6 fl oz / ^{3}/$_4$ cup)
Egg whites	60 g (2 oz)
Sugar	240 g (8^1/$_2$ oz)
Liquid glucose or corn syrup	240 g (8^1/$_2$ oz)
Water	90 ml (3 fl oz / 6 Tbsp)
Food colouring and flavouring of choice	as needed
Icing (confectioner's) sugar	as needed

Coating

Icing (confectioner's) sugar	100 g (3^1/$_2$ oz)
Corn flour (cornstarch)	100 g (3^1/$_2$ oz)

Brandy snap puddle

Butter	45 g (1^1/$_2$ oz)
Golden syrup	30 g (1 oz)
Sugar	35 g (1^1/$_4$ oz)
Plain (all-purpose) flour	20 g (^{2}/$_3$ oz)
Ground ginger	^{1}/$_2$ tsp
White sesame seeds	3 tsp, lightly toasted
Black sesame seeds	3 tsp

- **Marshmallows.** Start preparations at least a few hours, if not a day, ahead.

- In a heatproof bowl, add gelatine powder to cold water and leave to soak for 10 minutes. Before using, place bowl over a saucepan of simmering water so gelatine dissolves.

- Place egg whites into a clean grease-free mixing bowl. Using an electric mixer fitted with a whisk attachment, whisk egg whites until stiff peaks form.

- In the meantime, place sugar, glucose or corn syrup and water into a saucepan and bring to the boil until 127°C (260°F). Remove from heat and plunge saucepan into cold water to cool syrup.

- While egg whites are still whisking on low speed, slowly pour lightly cooled syrup into egg whites, then add gelatine solution. Divide mixture into a few batches, so you can have different colours and flavours. Add a few drops of food colouring and flavouring of choice to each batch and continue to whisk until mixture is stiff and thick.

- Spread each mixture onto individual baking trays lined with non-stick baking paper. Smooth out top with a palette knife or straight-edged plastic scraper. Using a sieve, dust generously with icing sugar. Leave to set for a few hours or overnight, then cut into cubes.

- **Coating.** Combine icing sugar and corn flour in a bowl. Add marshmallow cubes and toss well.

- **Brandy snap puddle.** Place butter, golden syrup and sugar into a bowl set over a saucepan of simmering water and gently melt together. Remove from heat.

- Sift flour and ground ginger together, then mix in sesame seeds. Add to melted butter and syrup mixture, mixing well. Pour mixture onto a baking tray lined with non-stick baking paper, spreading it out into a teardrop shape about 30 cm (12 in) long and 15 cm (6 in) wide at one end, tapering off to 5 cm (2 in) at the other end.

- Place tray into a preheated oven set at 180°C (350°F) and bake for about 5 minutes until dark golden brown in colour all the way through. Remove from oven, and allow to cool slightly before picking it up and bending it over a large upturned bowl, so it sits like a shell with a large flat base. Leave to cool.

- **To serve.** Carefully place brandy snap onto a large serving plate and arrange marshmallows on it. Serve.

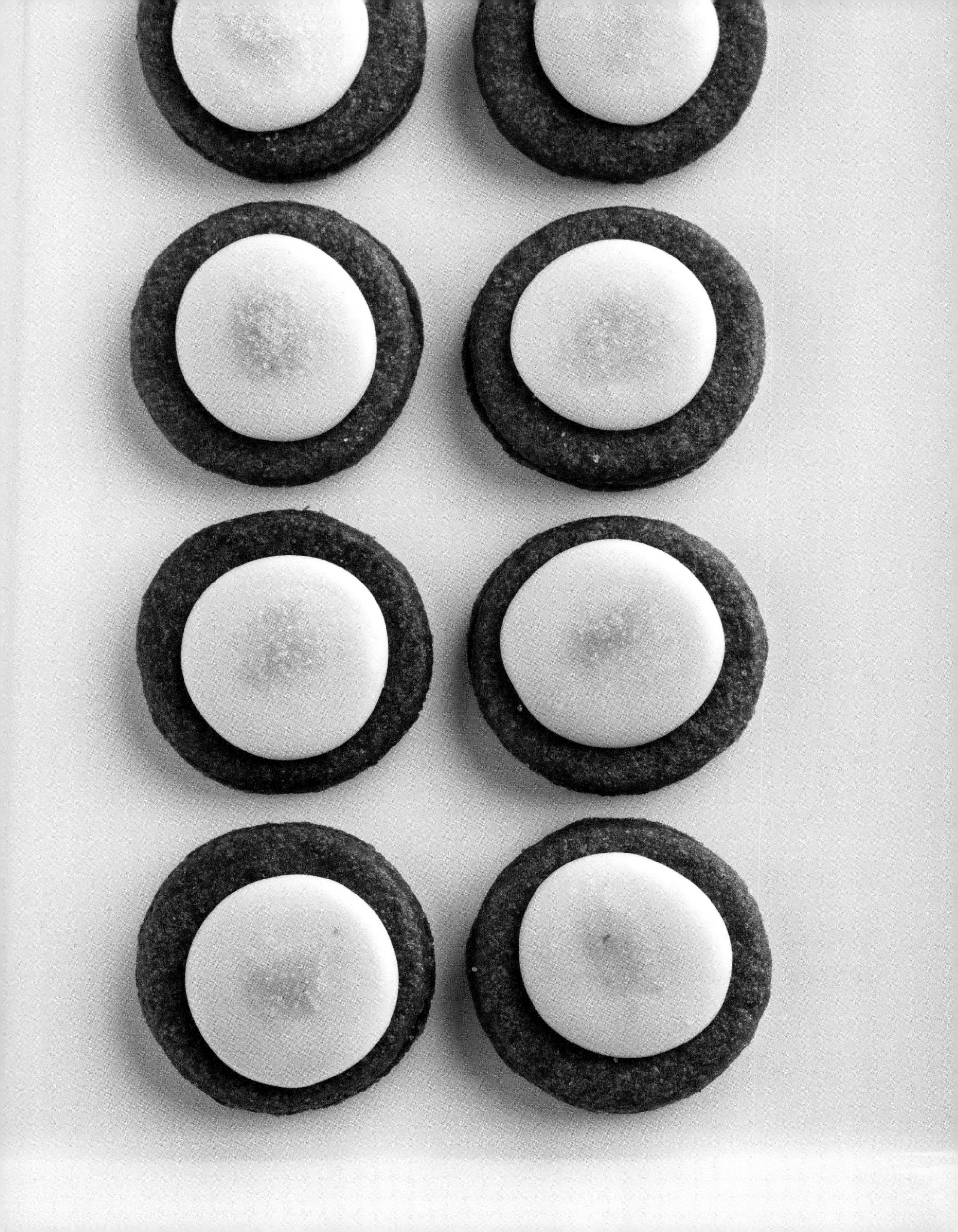

menu three

**Whipped Brie de Meaux & Crouton Mille-Feuille
with Balsamic Glaze & Arugula Salad**

Cauliflower Soup with Caviar
Wine: Sauvignon Blanc, New Zealand

★★★

**Char-grilled Atlantic Salmon with
Baby Spring Vegetables & Salsa Verde**
Wine: Cabernet Franc (less tannin)

**Chocolate & Raspberry Rice Pudding
with Baileys Crème Ganache**
Wine: Beerenauslese. Austria or Germany

★★★

Petite le Canelés de Bordeaux

Tea & Coffee

whipped brie de meaux & crouton mille-feuille with balsamic glaze & arugula salad *serves 4*

Whipping cheese might sound a little strange, but whipping works well with brie and Camembert or even a creamy blue cheese. This is really a cheese plate with crisp breads and is great served at the start of dinner. The balsamic glaze brings a nice acidic sweetness to the cheese. Ensure you take a fork full of everything on the plate, to really enjoy the different textures.

Balsamic reduction (page 204)	as needed

Croutons

Baguette	12 thin slices
Olive oil	as needed
Sea salt	to taste

Whipped brie

Ripe brie	350 g (12 oz), chilled, rind removed
Freshly ground black pepper	to taste

Arugula salad

Arugula (rocket) leaves	about 1 cup
Extra virgin olive oil	to taste
Sea salt	to taste

- **Croutons.** Prepare croutons a few hours ahead of serving. Brush both sides of baguette slices with olive oil and sprinkle with a little sea salt. Bake in preheated oven set at 150°C (300°F) for 10–15 minutes, or until golden brown and crisp. Leave to cool before storing in an airtight container until needed.

- **Whipped brie.** Place chilled brie into the bowl of an electric mixer fitted with a beater attachment and beat on medium speed until very white and creamy. Takes about 10 minutes. Stop mixer and scrape down sides of bowl 2–3 times while mixing. Store refrigerated until needed.

- **To serve.** Pour balsamic reduction into a squeeze bottle and draw an 'X' on one side of each serving plate.

- Remove brie from refrigerator and using 2 tablespoons dipped first in hot water, make 8 quenelles or small oval-shaped dollops of whipped brie. Quenelles or dollops should be about 1 tablespoonful in size. Place a quenelle of brie in the centre of a serving plate, then sprinkle with pepper and place a crouton on top. Arrange another quenelle on crouton, then sprinkle with pepper and top with another crouton. Repeat to make another 3 servings.

- **Arugula salad.** In a bowl, toss arugula with a little extra virgin olive oil and place a small pile at the side of each brie mille-feuille. Sprinkle with sea salt and serve.

korean corn & chilli bread *makes 8–10 loaves*

This bread has an interesting texture and a hint of sweetness from the sugar and sweetcorn. Spread with some butter and enjoy with a cool glass of Sauvignon Blanc.

Strong bread flour	160 g (5²/₃ oz)
Finely ground maize or polenta (almost powder-like)	120 g (4¹/₄ oz)
Sugar	60 g (2 oz)
Butter	60 g (2 oz), softened
Baking powder	15 g (¹/₂ oz)
Salt	5 g (¹/₆ oz)
Milk	80 ml (2²/₃ fl oz)
Eggs	2, small
Canned sweetcorn kernels	50 g (1²/₃ oz), drained and pat dry
Red chillies	10 g (¹/₃ oz), finely chopped
Egg wash	made by lightly beating 1 egg with 2 Tbsp water
Cold butter	27–30 small knobs

- Place all ingredients, except sweetcorn, chilles, egg wash and cold butter, into a mixing bowl. Combine mixture using a wooden spoon until dough is formed. Tip dough out onto a lightly floured work surface and knead for about 5 minutes.

- Add sweetcorn kernels and chillies, then gently mix into dough. The dough will be a little sticky due to the addition of the sweetcorn.

- Roughly mould dough into a ball and rest on a lightly floured work surface, covered with plastic wrap for 10–15 minutes. Divide rested dough into 8–10 equal parts.

- Mould each portion into a small, baton-shaped loaf with a fat middle and tapered ends. Place onto an oiled baking tray or a tray lined with non-stick baking paper. Using a sharp serrated knife, make a deep cut down the middle of each loaf.

- Lightly and evenly brush loaves with egg wash, then place 3 small knobs of butter along the inside each deep cut. Place tray into a preheated oven set at 190°C (370°F) and bake for 15–20 minutes. Remove from oven and place loaves onto a cooling rack. Consume within a day of making.

kitsch prawn cocktail *serves 4*

There is something cool about retro kitsch dishes! Long may they stand the test of time. This has to be one of the kings of kitsch dishes. It's lovely.

Romaine (cos) lettuce	200 g (7 oz), cleaned and sliced
Red wine vinaigrette	40 ml (1$^1/_3$ fl oz), made with 1 part red wine vinegar and 2 parts virgin olive oil
Tiger prawns (shrimps)	800 g (1$^3/_4$ lb), cooked and peeled
Quail's eggs	8, hard-boiled, peeled and halved
Dill	5 g ($^1/_6$ oz), chopped
Chervil	5 g ($^1/_6$ oz), chopped

Cocktail sauce

Mayonnaise (page 205)	300 g (11 oz)
Tomato sauce	150 g (5$^1/_3$ oz)
Brandy	5 tsp
Horse radish	25 g (1 oz)
Salt	to taste

Lemon crispy chips

Castor (superfine) sugar	30 g (1 oz)
Lemon juice	2 tsp
Water	2 Tbsp
Lemon	4 thin slices

- **Cocktail sauce.** Combine all ingredients in a small mixing bowl. Mix well, then set aside in the refrigerator.

- **Lemon crispy chips.** Place sugar, lemon juice and water into a saucepan over medium-low heat to make a syrup. Dip lemon slices into syrup to coat completely, then remove and arrange on a lined baking tray. Place in a preheated oven set at 120°C (250°F) to dry for about 1 hour. Check on lemon slices from time to time. Once completely dry and crisp, remove lemon slices.

- **To serve.** Place lettuce in a salad bowl and dress with red wine vinaigrette. Divide among 4 cocktail glasses, then arrange prawns on top. Drizzle with cocktail sauce and garnish with quail's eggs, dill, chervil and lemon crispy slice.

lobster, mussel & cod pot-au-feu with lemon grass, saffron & tomato jus *serves 4*

A classic way to prepare seafood, this recipe incorporates the light and bright flavours of the East, to please and delight the palate, while making the seafood dance.

Cooking oil	as needed
Fennel bulb	100 g (3^1/$_2$ oz), roughly diced
White onion	150 g (5^1/$_3$ oz), peeled and roughly diced
Celery	50 g (1^2/$_3$ oz), roughly diced
Ginger	10 g (^{1}/$_3$ oz), peeled and roughly diced
Garlic	15 g (^{1}/$_2$ oz), peeled and roughly diced
Tomato paste	50 g (1^2/$_3$ oz)
White wine	125 ml (4 fl oz / ^{1}/$_2$ cup)
Cherry tomatoes	500 g (1 lb 1^1/$_2$ oz)
Chicken stock (page 205)	250 ml (8 fl oz / 1 cup)
Lemon grass	20 g (^{2}/$_3$ oz), sliced
Cumin seeds	1 g (^{1}/$_{30}$ oz)
Thai sweet basil	15 g (^{1}/$_2$ oz)
Curry leaves	15 g (^{1}/$_2$ oz)
Curry powder	10 g (^{1}/$_3$ oz)
Salt	to taste
Ground black pepper	to taste
Boston lobsters	4, each about 600 g (1 lb 5^1/$_3$ oz)
Court boullion (page 205)	1 quantity
Clams	250 g (9 oz)
Black cod fillet	350 g (12 oz), cut into 3-cm (1-in) cubes
Scallops	10
Tiger prawns (shrimps)	250 g (9 oz), peeled, leaving tails intact
Butter	50 g (1^2/$_3$ oz)

- In a saucepan over medium heat, add some oil and sweat fennel, onion, celery, ginger and garlic. Add tomato paste and deglaze with white wine.

- Add cherry tomatoes, chicken stock, lemon grass, cumin, basil, curry leaves and curry powder. Cover and cook over low heat until tomatoes are soft, then check and adjust seasoning with salt and pepper to taste. Strain through a chinoise and set stock aside.

- Tie lobsters with string to keep them from curling when cooked. Bring court boullion to the boil in a pot and cook lobsters for 4 minutes. Remove and break off claws, then cook claws for another 1 minute. Shell, then cut lobster bodies into medaillons.

- Heat some oil in a pot and sweat clams, then add strained chicken stock. Cover and cook until clams open. Remove clams but retain stock in pot.

- In a frying pan, heat some oil and sear cod, scallops and prawns. Remove from heat. Arrange equal portions of seafood in 4 deep plates or bowls.

- Add butter to stock and stir to create a luxurious finish. Ladle over seafood. Garnish as desired. We used chervil and blanched kai lan. Bok choy and other leafy Asian vegetables will do as well.

espresso crème brûlée with espresso foam & nougatine spoon *serves 4*

This crème brûlée is divine. With each spoonful, I am transported to my favourite French café in Paris, where I sit, enjoying a latte. There are several layers of sophistication in this dessert — a smooth and creamy custard, an aromatic coffee flavour and taste, and light bubbles of coffee foam nestled on top of the caramelised coffee toffee. After you're done with dessert, enjoy nibbling on the almond nougatine spoon.

Espresso brûlée

Double (heavy) cream	350 ml (11⁴/₅ fl oz)
Whole milk (UHT is best)	150 ml (5 fl oz)
Double espresso coffee	50 ml (1²/₃ fl oz), if you don't have an espresso machine, get it from your nearest café
Kahlua liqueur	1 Tbsp
Egg yolks	6, from large eggs
Sugar	25 g (1 oz)
Coffee crystal sugar	4 Tbsp

Nougatine spoon

Sugar	100 g (3¹/₂ oz)
Lemon juice	a squeeze
Almond flakes	75 g (2¹/₃ oz), toasted

Espresso foam

Coffee	300 ml (10 fl oz / 1¹/₄ cups), made using a filter or coffee machine
Kahlua liqueur	80 ml (2²/₃ fl oz)
Sugar	40 g (1¹/₂ oz)
Soy lecithin	5 g (¹/₆ oz)

- **Espresso brûlée.** Use 150-ml (5-fl oz) ovenproof coffee cups. Lightly grease 4 such cups with butter and stand them on a baking tray. Set aside.

- Put cream and milk into a heavy-based saucepan and heat until just below boiling point, then stir in espresso and kahlua liqueur. Remove from heat and set aside.

- In a large bowl, whisk egg yolks and sugar until pale and creamy. Add hot coffee cream a third at a time, whisking well after each addition. Strain through a very fine sieve into a large pouring jug.

- Pour mixture into prepared coffee cups, dividing it up evenly. Carefully place into a preheated oven set at 150°C (300°F) and bake for 60–70 minutes, or until custard is lightly set on the top. To test if the custard is baked correctly, tilt cup slightly. Custard should come away from the side of the cup. The centre should remain a little wobbly. To double check, insert a sharp knife into custard and it should withdraw almost clean. The custard will continue to cook for a few minutes after it is out of the oven. Allow to cool a little at room temperature before chilling until required.

- **Nougatine spoon.** Place sugar with a squeeze of lemon juice into a heavy-based frying pan. Make a dry caramel by stirring constantly over medium heat with a wooden spoon until light golden in colour.

- Add toasted almond flakes and immediately tip onto a lightly oiled work surface and roll to a thickness of about 0.3-cm (1/8-in). Working quickly while nougatine is still hot, cut out 4 teaspoon shapes and place separately over teaspoons to mould. Store in an airtight container until needed. If nougatine hardens before you are able to complete working with it, place it on a baking tray lined with non-stick paper and reheat in the oven.

- **To serve.** Remove brûlées from refrigerator 30 minutes before serving to allow them to warm up a little. Sprinkle about 1 Tbsp coffee crystal sugar over the top of each brûlée, then use a gas blowtorch to caramelise sugar. Allow to harden.

- In the meantime, prepare expresso foam. Place coffee, kahlua and sugar in a pot and bring to the boil. Remove from heat and stir in soy lecithin. Using a hand-held blender, create foam from mixture. Spoon foam over brûlées and place cups on a saucer. Arrange nougatine spoon on the side.

Balsamic reduction
(page 204)   as needed

Basil syrup (page 203)   as needed

Puff pastry mille-feuille

Puff pastry (page 202)   3 sheets

Icing (confectioner's)
sugar   as needed

Lemon cream filling

Sugar   120 g (4$^1/_4$ oz)

Lemons   2, grated for zest
and juice extracted

Egg yolks   4

Butter   60 g (2 oz)

Semi whipped cream   300 g (11 oz)

Berry compote

Firm strawberries   400 g (14$^1/_3$ oz), hulled
and cut into small cubes

Raspberry coulis
(page 203)   150 ml (5 fl oz)

Gin jelly cubes

Gelatine leaves   3 sheets

Water   180 ml (6 fl oz / $^3/_4$ cup)

Sugar   60 g (2 oz)

Gin   100 ml (3$^1/_2$ fl oz)

- **Puff pastry mille-feuille.** Roll puff pastry sheets to 0.3-cm ($^1/_8$-in) thickness. Using a fork, prick a holes all over sheets, then leave to rest a while. Cut pastry into 12 rectangles, each 10 x 4-cm (4 x 1$^1/_2$-in) and place slightly apart on a baking tray lined with non-stick baking paper. Sprinkle lightly with icing sugar, then cover with non-stick baking paper and place another baking tray on top to weigh pastry down. Place in a preheated oven set at 220°C (440°F) and bake until glazed and golden brown. Remove from oven. Set aside to cool.

- **Lemon cream filling.** In a heatproof bowl, stir together lemon juice, zest and egg yolks with a hand whisk until combined. Do not introduce air into mixture. Set mixture over a pan of simmering water and gently whisk until mixture thickens, adding butter halfway through. Takes about 5 minutes. Take care not to allow mixture to get too hot or eggs will be cooked. Once thickened, cover with plastic wrap and refrigerate to cool. When cool, fold in whipped cream and whisk until firm. Cover and refrigerate until required.

- **Berry compote.** Place strawberry cubes in a bowl. Add raspberry coulis and mix well, then cover and refrigerate until ready to use.

- **Gin jelly cubes.** Line a baking tray or a large flat shallow dish with plastic wrap.

- Soak gelatine sheets in a bowl of cold water to soften. Squeeze to remove excess water before using.

- In a small saucepan, bring water to the boil with sugar. Remove from heat and add softened gelatine sheets, stirring to dissolve. Set aside to cool before stirring in gin. Pour mixture into prepared baking tray or dish. The mixture should be no more than 0.75-cm ($^1/_3$-in) high. Refrigerate until set, then cut into small cubes.

- **To serve.** Spoon lemon cream filling into a piping bag and pipe some lemon cream onto a pastry rectangle. Top with another pastry rectangle, then repeat to pipe with lemon cream and layer with another pastry rectangle. You now have 3 layers of pastry and 2 layers of cream. Make another 3 mille-feuille with remaining cream and pastry.

- Dust top of mille-feuille with icing sugar and transfer to serving plates. Arrange some gin jelly cubes alongside mille-feuille, together with some basil syrup, balsamic reduction and berry compote.

orange tuiles *makes 30*

Orange julienne strips

Orange	1
Sugar	100 g (3^1/$_2$ oz)
Water	100 ml (3^1/$_2$ fl oz)

Tuile paste

Plain (all-purpose) flour	75 g (2^1/$_3$ oz)
Icing (confectioner's) sugar	75 g (2^1/$_3$ oz)
Egg whites	75 g (2^1/$_3$ oz), lightly beaten
Butter	75 g (2^1/$_3$ oz), melted

You can shape these tuiles any way you like. Lay them over small bowls or inside small fluted tart moulds, so they harden in the form of little baskets which you can fill just before serving. Try piping in sweetened and whipped fresh cream, then topping with strawberries, blueberries or raspberries, and dust with icing sugar.

- **Orange julienne strips.** Julienne (finely slice) zest from orange. In a small saucepan, bring sugar and water to the boil. Add orange zest and boil until soft. Drain and pat dry with kitchen paper.

- **Tuile paste.** Sift flour and icing sugar into a medium bowl. Using a wooden spoon, stir in egg whites and mix well, then add melted butter and mix into a smooth paste. Scrape down sides of bowl and cover with plastic wrap. Leave paste for 1 hour.

- Make a stencil out of a flat piece of plastic, about 0.1-cm (^{1}/$_{25}$-in). I used the classic round shape about 6 cm (2^1/$_2$ in) in diameter, but you can choose any shape you desire. Place stencil onto a baking tray lined with non-stick baking paper, then place a spoonful of tuile paste onto stencil. With a palette knife, spread paste evenly until levelled with stencil. Peel off stencil. Place orange strips on tuile to decorate. Repeat to make 2–3 tuiles each time.

- Place baking tray into a preheated oven set at 180°C (350°F) and bake tuiles for 5–10 minutes. The edges will colour and the middle will remain pale. Remove baked tuiles with a palette knife and quickly shape over a thin rolling pin or any other shape to set. Store in an airtight container until needed.

menu three

Sun-dried Tomato Ciabatta with
Extra Virgin Olive Oil & Balsamic Vinegar

Smoked Salmon Terrine with Keta Caviar,
White Anchovy & Fingerling Potato Salad
Wine: Pinot Gris, Alsace

Lobster Cannelloni with Seared Snapper,
Parsley Purée & White Tomato Foam
Wine: Pinot Grigio

Almond & Walnut Tartlet with Toffee Sauce
& Chocolate Chip Ice Cream
Wine: Sauternes

Citron & Raspberry Macarons

★★★

Tea & Coffee

sun-dried tomato ciabatta with extra virgin olive oil & balsamic vinegar makes 2–3 loaves

Ciabatta has become popular all over the world, given its versatility. It goes well with many pasta dishes and sauces, and can also be filled with gourmet ingredients, then toasted in a panini grill. I enjoy simply dipping it into aged balsamic vinegar, then good extra virgin olive oil for the simple but complex flavours. The high water content in this recipe gives the ciabatta its open-hole chewy crumb. Don't be surprised that a cake beater is used in making this bread.

Biga ferment

Strong bread flour	225 g (8 oz)
Wholemeal (wholewheat) flour	20 g (^{2}/$_3$ oz)
Instant active dry yeast	1 g (^{1}/$_{30}$ oz)
Cold water	135 ml (4^1/$_2$ fl oz)

Dough

Strong bread flour	245 g (8^2/$_3$ oz)
Instant active dry yeast	2 g (^{1}/$_{15}$ oz)
Salt	10 g (^{1}/$_3$ oz)
Cold water	255 ml (8 fl oz / 1 cup)
Sun-dried tomatoes	50 g (1^2/$_3$ oz), drained and cut into small strips
Ice cubes	4–5

- **Biga ferment.** Start preparations a day ahead. Place all ingredients for ferment into a mixing bowl and mix well until elastic in texture. Place into an oiled container, cover and leave to ferment overnight (18–24 hours) at room temperature. This dough should be firm.

- **Dough.** Place all ingredients, except sun-dried tomatoes and ice cubes, into the bowl of an electric mixer fitted with a beater attachment. Mix on low speed until a rough dough is formed, then increase to medium speed until dough is smooth, silky and almost fully developed. Takes about 5 minutes. You may need to scrape down the bowl from time to time to ensure dough is mixed thoroughly. Add sun-dried tomatoes and gently mix in.

- Place dough into an oiled rectangular container large enough for dough to double in bulk. Cover with plastic wrap and leave for 20 minutes. Gently deflate gassed dough by folding it onto itself 2–3 times, using plenty of dusting flour in the container. Rest for another 20 minutes.

- Gently deflate gassed dough again by folding it onto itself 2–3 times, again using plenty of dusting flour in the container. Rest for another 20 minutes.

- Gently deflate gassed dough a third time by folding it onto itself 2–3 times, again using plenty of dusting flour in the container. Rest for another 30 minutes undisturbed. Notice how the dough has firmed up?

- Turn dough out onto a well floured work surface. Using a dough scraper, cut dough into 2–3 rectangles. Try to handle dough as little as possible as rough handling will result in loss of air and gas bubbles, essential to the texture of ciabatta. Loosely roll each rectangle in flour so that the top surface is covered in flour. Place onto a well floured tea towel with the top surface facing up. Leave to rise for 30 minutes.

- Preheat oven to 230°C (450°F). Place a baking tray or baking stone inside oven, together with a small ovenproof dish on the bottom shelf.

- Pick up dough pieces from floured tea towel and gently stretch them before placing onto a baking tray lined with non-stick baking paper. Slide dough, still on the non-stick baking paper, directly onto hot baking tray or baking stone, and place ice cubes into a small ovenproof dish. Do all this quickly and close oven door.

- Bake for 30–35 minutes, or until ciabatta is a dark golden brown colour and produces a hollow sound when tapped on the bottom. Remove from oven and place on a cooling rack.

- **To serve.** Slice and serve with extra virgin olive oil and balsamic vinegar.

Terrines may come in and out of vogue, but they always come back. Smoked salmon is one that will always have my heart, and the addition of salmon roe brings a lovely seasoning element.

smoked salmon terrine with keta caviar, white anchovy *&* fingerling potato salad *serves 4*

Dill and honey mustard dressing (page 209)	50 ml (1²/₃ fl oz)
Keta caviar	60 g (2 oz)
White anchovies	4, cut into small pieces
Dill leaves	as needed

Smoked salmon terrine

Salmon fillets	400 g (14¹/₃ oz)
Smoked salmon	200 g (7 oz)
Lemon	1, juice extracted
Salt	to taste
Single (light) cream	200 ml (6¹/₂ fl oz)
Salt	to taste
Ground black pepper	to taste

Fingerling potato salad

Beef bouillon powder or stock cube	5 g (¹/₆ oz)
White wine vinegar	4 tsp
Dijon mustard	5 g (¹/₆ oz)
Extra virgin olive oil	1 Tbsp
Mayonnaise (page 205)	20 g (²/₃ oz)
Finely chopped parsley	1 tsp
Finely chopped chives	1 tsp
Finely chopped dill	1 tsp
Fingerling potatoes	10
Bacon	50 g (1²/₃ oz), chopped
Salt	to taste
Ground black pepper	to taste

bread cases with olive tapenade & oven-roasted tomato with crisp green salad serves 4

This is a great way to use up day-old bread. With its Mediterranean flavour, this can also be served as a light summer lunch. The olive tapenade, oven-roasted tomatoes and crusty bread cases make a perfect combination.

Olive tapenade (page 210)	½ quantity

Oven-roasted tomatoes

Tomatoes	3, medium
Extra virgin olive oil	as needed
Sea salt flakes	to taste
Freshly ground black pepper	to taste
Sugar	a pinch

Bread cases

Quality bread (sourdough if available)	6 slices
Butter	as needed, softened

Garnish

Sour cream	100 g (3½ oz)
Green salad leaves	as needed
Extra virgin olive oil	as needed
Walnuts	150 g (5⅓ oz), roasted

- **Oven-roasted tomatoes.** Wash tomatoes, then cut in half and remove stems. Place tomatoes, cut side up, on a grilling rack or wire rack with a baking tray underneath. Brush tomatoes generously with olive oil, then sprinkle with salt flakes, pepper and sugar to neutralise the acidity. Place tomatoes into a preheated oven set at 180°C (350°F) and bake for about 1 hour until edges of tomatoes start to brown. Remove and set aside to cool.

- **Bread cases.** Remove and discard bread crust. Using a rolling pin, flatten bread, then cut out 4 circles, each about 11 cm (4½ in) in diameter. Lightly butter one side, then push into a standard size muffin tin, buttered side down. Place into a preheated oven set at 200°C (400°F) and bake for 10–15 minutes, until crisp and golden brown.

- **To serve.** Place each bread case onto a large serving plate. Spoon 1½ Tbsp tapenade into each case and top with a roasted tomato and a dollop or quenelle of sour cream. (Spoon tapenade into bread cases just before serving or cases will go soft.) Serve with a simple crisp green salad, dressed with extra virgin olive, and walnuts.

Warm goat's cheese is one of life's good things. Here, it is crusted with toasted nuts and seeds, making a winning combination. Setting the grilled capsicum in a clear tomato terrine is a lovely touch, and easier to do than it may seem.

warm nut-crusted goat's cheese crouton with capsicum-tomato terrine & aubergine purée *serves 4*

Aubergine purée (page 208)	60 g (2 oz)
Pesto sauce (page 204)	50 g (1²/₃ oz)
Tomato confit (page 210)	40 g (1¹/₂ oz)

Capsicum-tomato terrine

Tomatoes	500 g (1 lb 1¹/₂ oz), quartered
Salt	to taste
Tabasco sauce	to taste
Gelatine leaves	11 sheets
Yellow and red capsicums (bell peppers)	500 g (1 lb 1¹/₂ oz) each

Goat's cheese crouton

Baguette	1
Goat's cheese	300 g (11 oz)
Sliced almonds	20 g (²/₃ oz)
Pumpkin seeds	30 g (1 oz)
Black and white sesame seeds	15 g (¹/₂ oz) each

Salad

Arugula (rocket) leaves	40 g (1¹/₂ oz)
Chervil	5 g (¹/₆ oz)
Basil leaves	5 g (¹/₆ oz)
Vinaigrette	as needed

- **Capsicum-tomato terrine.** Start preparations a day ahead. Process tomatoes in a blender, then pour mixture into a clean muslin cloth. Tie edges of cloth up, then hang over a bowl to collect the clear juice. Leave overnight.

- The following day, place tomato juice in a pan and season with salt and a hint of Tabasco sauce. Soak gelatine leaves in cold water until soft. Squeeze out excess water, then add to pan and mix well. Place over low heat, stirring until gelatine is melted. Remove from heat.

- Wash and dry capsicums. Brush with a little oil and grill until skins are black and blistered. Remove from grill and allow to cool until they can be handled, then peel off skins. Wash off any bits left behind. Spread capsicums on a baking tray and roast on low heat to soften. When ready, leave to cool slightly, then pull capsicums apart into strips.

- Lightly oil a terrine mould. Line with plastic wrap and alternately layer tomato juice jelly with capsicum strips. Cover and refrigerate to set. To serve, turn terrine out of mould and slice evenly with a hot knife.

- **Goat's cheese crouton.** Cut baguette into thick slices, roughly 4 x 1 cm (1½ x ½ in) and toast. Shape goat's cheese into 4 discs, each about 2-cm (1-in) thick and the same diameter as baguette.

- Place almonds and pumpkin seeds in a plastic bag and crush with a rolling pin. Mix with sesame seeds and toast in a dry frying pan. Transfer to a bowl, add a little olive oil and mix well. Coat goat's cheese discs with nut mixture and place one on each baguette slice. Arrange on a baking tray, then bake in a preheated 160°C (325°F) oven until warm and soft, but still holding its shape.

- **To serve.** Spoon some aubergine purée and pesto sauce across each serving plate. I made three lines of each across a square plate.

- Dress salad leaves with vinaigrette and arrange in the middle of plate. Place goat's cheese crouton at one corner of plate and a slice of terrine in an opposite corner. Top terrine with tomato confit.

grilled portobello mushrooms layered with fennel pollen polenta & aubergine purée with cucumber & yellow capsicum foam *serves 4*

Portobello mushrooms are one of my favourites. In this recipe, they can be replaced with any good field mushroom. A must-try is the polenta cake. It is so versatile, you can enjoy it with other dishes as well.

Cucumber and yellow capsicum foam (page 207)	as needed
Aubergine purée (page 208)	as needed

Grilled mushrooms

Portobello mushrooms	600 g (1 lb 5^1/$_3$ oz)
Balsamic vinegar	50 ml (1^2/$_3$ fl oz)
Salt	to taste
Ground black pepper	to taste
Virgin olive oil	100 ml (3^1/$_3$ fl oz)

Fennel pollen polenta

Milk	500 ml (16 fl oz / 2 cups)
Butter	50 g (1^2/$_3$ oz)
Salt	to taste
Ground black pepper	to taste
Ground nutmeg	a pinch
Polenta	250 g (9 oz)
Garlic	1 clove, peeled and chopped
Thyme	a sprig, chopped
Marjoram	a few sprigs, chopped
Fennel pollen (powdered fennel)	10 g (^{1}/$_3$ oz)
Fennel purée (page 209)	50 g (1^2/$_3$ oz)

Capsicums

Red and yellow capsicums (bell peppers)	1 each, roasted and skins removed
Olive oil	as needed
Salt	to taste
Ground black pepper	to taste

- **Grilled mushrooms.** Marinate mushrooms with balsamic vinegar, salt, pepper and olive oil. When ready to serve, grill mushrooms, then slice into big chunks at an angle. Reserve marinade.

- **Fennel pollen polenta.** In a saucepan, boil milk with butter, then season with salt, pepper and nutmeg. Stir in polenta and bring to the boil. Add chopped garlic, thyme, marjoram and fennel pollen and boil until polenta is soft. Add fennel purée and boil until it firms up again. Pour into a container or loaf tin, the width of portobello mushrooms and leave to cool. When ready to serve, cut into 1-cm (1/2-in) thick slices and pan-fry until golden.

- **Capsicums.** Wash and dry capsicums. Brush with a little oil and grill until skins are black and blistered. Remove from grill, allow to cool until they can be handled, then peel off skins. Wash off any bits left behind, then cut in half and remove pith and seeds. Cut into strips. Toss in a hot pan with olive oil, salt and pepper.

- **Aubergine purée.** Warm purée in a small pot. If it starts to dry out, add a bit of olive oil and butter until original consistency is restored.

- **To serve.** Spoon aubergine purée across each serving plate. I made three lines across a rectangular plate. Layer mushrooms and polenta to create a stack in the centre of each plate. Top with roasted capsicums and reserved marinade. Spoon cucumber and yellow capsicum foam around plate.

rosé wine jelly with summer berries *serves 4*

A delightful dessert packed with the simple flavours and tastes of rosé wine and summer berries. Rosé wine may be substituted with champagne or any good quality sparkling wine. Serve with a tuile biscuit if desired.

Gelatine leaves	8 sheets
Rosé wine	750 ml (24 fl oz / 3 cups)
Castor (superfine) sugar	600 g (1 lb 5$\frac{1}{3}$ oz)
Strawberries	6, small, cut into quarters
Fresh raspberries	6 Tbsp
Fresh blueberries	6 Tbsp

- Soak gelatine sheets in cold water for 10 minutes, then squeeze out excess water before use.

- In a large heavy-based saucepan, heat wine with sugar until syrup reaches boiling point. Remove from heat and stir in gelatine leaves until dissolved. Transfer to a large cooling jug and leave until lukewarm.

- Pour a 1-cm ($\frac{1}{2}$-in) layer of jelly into 4 small serving glasses, then refrigerate until just starting to set. Remove from refrigerator and arrange berries evenly over layer of setting jelly. Pour in more liquid jelly. Refrigerate overnight.

- **To serve.** Remove glasses from refrigerator 10 minutes before serving.

almond & rosemary biscotti *makes 50*

Biscotti are simple cookie bars that are lightly baked, then sliced and baked again. Almonds are a classic ingredient. I have added rosemary to impart a light perfume. Enjoy with coffee.

Blanched or skinned almonds	100 g (3^1/$_2$ oz)
Castor (superfine) sugar	150 g (5^1/$_3$ oz)
Plain (all-purpose) flour	150 g (5^1/$_3$ oz)
Baking powder	2 tsp
Eggs	2
Butter	1 Tbsp, softened
Vanilla essence	^{1}/$_4$ tsp
Finely chopped rosemary	1 tsp

• Place almonds onto a baking tray and toast in a preheated oven set at 180°C (350°F) until pale amber in colour. Remove and set aside to cool.

• Sift sugar, flour and baking powder together into a large mixing bowl. Add eggs, softened butter, vanilla essence, almonds and rosemary. Mix using a wooden spoon until a dough forms.

• With floured hands, divide dough in half. On a lightly floured work surface, roll each half of dough into a log shape 3–5-cm (1–2-in) wide. Transfer logs to a lined baking tray, spacing them 5 cm (2 in) apart, as logs will spread during baking. Bake in a preheated oven set at 170°C (330°F) for about 20 minutes, or until firm to the touch. Remove from oven and leave to cool on a wire rack for about 10 minutes.

• Transfer logs to a cutting board and, using a serrated knife, cut logs on the diagonal into 0.5-cm (^{1}/$_4$-in) thick slices. Arrange evenly on a baking tray.

• Lower oven temperature to 120°C (250°F) and bake biscotti slices for 10 minutes. Turn slices over and bake for another 10 minutes, or until firm to the touch. Remove from oven and leave to cool. Store in an airtight container until needed.

• **To serve.** Serve with coffee or tea at the end of the meal.

chocolate & nut panforte

makes one 20-cm (8-in) round cake

Hazelnuts	135 g (4¾ oz)
Blanched almonds	135 g (4¾ oz)
Candied mango strips	50 g (1⅔ oz), cut into ½-cm (¼-in) bits
Candied pineapple rings	50 g (1⅔ oz), cut into small segments
Dried apricots	50 g (1⅔ oz), cut into ½-cm (¼-in) thick slices
Finely chopped mixed peel	65 g (2⅓ oz)
Cocoa powder	15 g (½ oz)
Strong bread flour	75 g (2⅓ oz)
Sugar	95 g (3⅓ oz)
Honey	130 g (4½ oz)
Dark chocolate	65 g (2⅓ oz), melted
Icing (confectioner's) sugar, optional	

Panforte is a specialty from Siena, Italy. In Italian, "pane" means "bread" and "forte" means "strong", aptly describing this rather "strong bread". This was what the Italian soldiers carried around in their army packs during wartime, as it was sturdy and robust enough to withstand rough treatment. Just a small slice with some coffee gave the soldiers renewed energy. The classic panforte is made without chocolate and eaten at Christmas time, but I have added chocolate because the combination works so well. You can also experiment with a variety of dried fruit such as dried papaya or shredded coconut.

- Line a 20-cm (8-in) loose-bottomed cake tin with non-stick baking paper. Set aside.

- Place hazelnuts on a baking tray, then toast in oven for 10–15 minutes. Remove and cool before rubbing hazelnuts in a clean tea towel to remove skins. Place blanched almonds on a baking tray, then toast in oven until a very pale golden colour. Takes 10–15 minutes. Take care not to overcook nuts, as they will continue to cook for a few minutes after they leave the oven. Coarsely chop hazelnut and almonds.

- Mix nuts, fruit, mixed peel, cocoa powder and bread flour well together in a large bowl.

- Place sugar and honey in a heavy-based saucepan and cook over medium heat until mixture reaches 116°C–118°C (240°F–244°F) on a candy thermometer. Alternatively, drop a little of the syrup into cold water and it should form a ball when rubbed between your fingers. This is known as the soft ball stage.

- Remove syrup from heat and stir in melted chocolate until well combined. Immediately pour chocolate syrup into nut and fruit mixture, stirring quickly with a wooden spoon until mixture is well combined. Working quickly, place mixture into prepared cake tin. Dip your hand in warm water, then pat mixture down until it is somewhat smooth and level. The mixture will cool quickly and become very stiff, so work very fast.

- Place cake tin onto a baking tray and into a preheated oven set at 180°C (350°F). Bake for 20–25 minutes. The panforte won't colour or seem very firm even after baking, but it will harden as it cools. Leave to cool in tin until firm.

- **To serve.** Remove panforte from tin and peel off baking paper. Cut panforte into thin wedges and dust with icing sugar, if desired. Serve with coffee or tea.

menu three

Smoked Paprika & Sunflower Dinner Rolls with Antipasto

★★★

**Shaved Spring Vegetable Salad
in Sake & Ginger Shoot Dressing**
Wine: Pinot Gris or Sauvignon Blanc, France

★★★

**Pappardelle with Char-grilled Aubergine,
Courgette & Capsicum on Tomato & Basil Ragout**
Wine: Red Bordeaux, Margaux

★★★

**Carrot Cake with Cream Cheese Icing, Sweet Basil Dressing
& Caramelised Poached Baby Carrots
with Orange & Lemon Candied Peel**
Wine: Sauternes

★★★

Trio of Chocolate-dipped Cherries

★★★

Tea & Coffee

smoked paprika & sunflower dinner rolls with antipasto *makes about 30 rolls*

These little rolls are frequently on the bread menu of The Providores in London. It is owned by my good friend, Peter Gordon, a fellow Kiwi. Where possible, use sweet smoked paprika. You will notice the difference. And it goes wonderfully with the antipasto platter.

Rolls

Strong bread flour	500 g (1 lb 1½ oz)
Salt	10 g (⅓ oz)
Sugar	10 g (⅓ oz)
Instant active dried yeast	5 g (⅙ oz)
Olive oil	2 tsp
Sunflower seeds	160 g (5⅔ oz)
Ground paprika (sweet smoked, if available)	10 g (⅓ oz)
Water	300 ml (10 fl oz / 1¼ cups), or a little more
Ice cubes	4–5

Chilled antipasto

Kalamata black olives	100 g (3½ oz)
Artichokes hearts	4, good-size, cooked and marinated in olive oil and herbs
Onion jam (page 138)	
Sun-dried tomatoes	100 g (3½ oz)
Grilled aubergines (eggplants)	
Grilled capsicums (bell peppers)	
Arugula (rocket) leaves	30 g (1 oz)

- **Rolls.** Start preparation for rolls a day ahead.

- Place bread flour, salt, sugar, yeast and olive oil in a large mixing bowl and mix into a dough using a wooden spoon. Tip dough out onto a lightly floured work surface and knead for 10–15 minutes, taking a 30-second rest every 2–3 minutes, until dough is smooth and elastic. Add sunflower seeds and mix until evenly combined.

- Lightly oil a bowl large enough to allow dough to double in bulk. Put dough into bowl and cover with plastic wrap. Leave in a warm place for 1 hour until dough doubles in bulk. Gently fold dough back onto itself, causing it to deflate slightly, but this will help dough develop more strength. Cover again with plastic wrap and leave for 30 minutes.

- Deflate dough again by repeating the folding process. Cover with lightly oiled plastic wrap, then refrigerate overnight.

- The following day, gently tip dough out onto a lightly floured work surface and divide it into 30 equal pieces, each about 40 g (1¹/₂ oz). Roll each dough piece into a small ball, then shape as desired. Place 10 rolls each on a baking tray lined with non-stick baking paper. Cover with a sheet of plastic and leave for 1–1¹/₂ hours to rise. Dough should be slightly active to the touch and a little under-proved. Test by pressing dough lightly with a finger. It should spring back. If you like, dust rolls with flour, then use a sharp pointed pair of scissors or knife to make three diagonal cuts in each roll.

- Place rolls into a preheated oven set at 220°C (440°F) with a small ovenproof dish on the bottom shelf. Quickly place 4–5 ice cubes into heated ovenproof dish to create steam. Bake for 15–18 minutes. Remove rolls from oven and place on to a wire rack to cool.

- To reheat rolls, place on a baking tray and bake in a preheated oven set at 200°C (400°F) for 5–8 minutes until warm and crisp.

- **To serve.** Serve rolls with a selection of chilled antipasto.

shaved spring vegetable salad in sake & ginger shoot dressing *serves 4*

Every time I feel like eating extra healthy, I whip up one of these little salads. The subtle Japanese flavours bring the vegetables to life. Top the salad with some shaved dry bonito flakes, if desired.

Green asparagus	8 spears
Baby carrots	8
Pea pods	8
Stem lettuce (*woh sun*)	40 g (1$\frac{1}{2}$ oz)
Cucumber	1
Yellow and green courgette (zucchini)	1 each
Cherry tomatoes	4
Red radish	1
Chives	15 g ($\frac{1}{2}$ oz), chopped
White sesame seeds	10 g ($\frac{1}{3}$ oz)

Dressing

Japanese ginger shoots	15 g ($\frac{1}{2}$ oz)
Olive oil	8 tsp
Sesame oil	4 tsp
Sake	1 Tbsp
White balsamic vinegar	4 tsp
White wine vinegar	2 tsp

- Wash vegetables. Blanch asparagus, carrots, pea pods and stem lettuce in a pot of boiling water, then quickly refresh in iced water to stop the cooking process. Thinly slice.

- Thinly slice raw cucumber, courgettes and radish using a mandolin. Halve tomatoes.

- Prepare dressing. Slice ginger and reserve a slice for garnish. Bruise ginger lightly using a mortar and pestle. Mix with olive and sesame oils, sake and vinegars.

- Toss vegetables and chives with dressing and arrange in serving bowls. Sprinkle sesame seeds over. Cut remaining slice of ginger and use as garnish.

beef rendang curry with braised cabbage & coconut foam *serves 4*

Rendang is a wonderful beef dish from Indonesia, and this recipe offers a fantastic twist with classic ingredients and new elements. Prepare double the portion, then enjoy the leftovers the following day. The flavours will mature overnight, and it will taste even better.

Coconut foam (page 207), optional	
Coconut rice (page 210)	1 quantity

Rendang paste

Cooking oil	100 ml (3¹/₃ fl oz)
Shallots	200 g (7 oz), peeled and finely chopped
Garlic	70 g (2¹/₂ oz), peeled and finely chopped
Galangal	40 g (1¹/₂ oz)
Prawn (shrimp) paste (*belacan*)	15 g (¹/₂ oz)
Dried prawns (shrimps)	80 g (2⁴/₅ oz)
Ground turmeric	3 g (¹/₁₀ oz)
Coriander seeds	9 g (¹/₃ oz)
Cumin seeds	17 g (¹/₂ oz)
Red chillies	330 g (11²/₃ oz), sliced
Lemon grass	85 g (3 oz)
Lime juice	7 tsp
Kaffir lime juice	4 tsp
Kaffir lime leaves	12 g (¹/₂ oz), sliced
Water	1 litre (32 fl oz / 4 cups)

Beef cheeks & fillet

Cooking oil	50 ml (1²/₃ fl oz)
Beef cheeks	1 kg (2 lb 3 oz)
Coconut milk	1.4 litres (45¹/₂ fl oz)
Fish sauce	2 tsp
Beef fillet	4 slices, each about 80 g (2⁴/₅ oz)

Braised cabbage

Butter	50 g (1²/₃ oz)
Onion	50 g (1²/₃ oz), peeled and shredded
Cabbage	200 g (7 oz), shredded
Chicken stock (page 205), optional	50 ml (1²/₃ fl oz)
Salt	to taste
Ground white pepper	to taste

- *Rendang* **paste.** Heat oil in a deep frying pan and sweat shallots and garlic over low heat. Add remaining ingredients for paste and braise for 30 minutes. Remove from heat, transfer to a blender and purée until fine. Store in a sterilised jar.

- **Beef cheeks & fillet.** Heat oil in a pan and sear beef cheeks on both sides until brown and partially crispy. Place beef cheeks in an ovenproof pot. Add coconut milk and 300 g (11 oz) *rendang* paste. Cover and braise for 2 hours in an oven set at 120°C (250°F) until very tender. Remove from oven.

- Remove cheeks from sauce and set aside. Pass sauce through a fine mesh sieve into a mixing bowl, then season with salt, pepper and fish sauce to taste. There should be at least 100 ml (3^{1}/$_{3}$ fl oz) sauce. Add beef fillet and leave to marinate for at least 30 minutes. Heat a pan and sear beef fillet to desired doneness. Leave to rest in a warm place while assembling rest of dish. Reserve sauce.

- **Braised cabbage.** Melt butter in a frying pan and sweat onion. Add cabbage and stir-fry. Add chicken stock only if mixture is dry, as cabbage has a high water content. When cabbage is soft, season with salt and pepper to taste. Set aside.

- **To serve.** Ensure all components of dish are hot. Spoon *rendang* sauce onto serving plates, then arrange braised cabbage in the centre. Top with beef fillet and cheeks. If feeling ambitious, top with coconut foam (not shown in photo). Otherwise, simply garnish with julienne chilli and coriander leaves. Serve with coconut rice.

lemon curd & raspberry meringue shots *serves 4*

Two powerful desserts and an iced espresso shot is enough to finish anyone off. Combining the lemon curd and raspberry compote with a smooth sweet meringue is an ideal way to have three taste sensations in one mouthful. Just slide your spoon down the side of the glass. Next, move on to the strawberry soup infused with aniseed and goat's cheese ice cream on a biscuit. Enjoy the components individually or allow the ice cream to melt into the soup, then dip the biscuit in, stir and swallow. Finish off with a shot of iced espresso with simple sugar syrup added for some sweetness.

Lemon curd

Sugar	120 g (4½ oz)
Lemons	2, medium, grated for zest and juice extracted
Egg yolks	4
Butter	60 g (2 oz)

Raspberry conserve

Fresh or frozen raspberries	100 g (3½ oz)
Sugar	1 tsp
Corn flour (cornstarch)	¼ tsp, mixed with 1 tsp cold water

Meringue

Egg whites	2
Castor (superfine) sugar	110 g (4 oz)

- **Lemon curd.** In a bowl, stir together sugar, lemon zest and juice and egg yolks with a hand whisk until combined. Do not introduce any air into mixture. Set over a saucepan of simmering water and gently whisk until mixture thickens, adding butter halfway through. Takes about 5 minutes. Do not allow mixture to get too hot or eggs will scramble. Once lemon curd is thick, cover with plastic wrap and refrigerate to cool.

- **Raspberry conserve.** Place raspberries and sugar into a small saucepan and place over medium heat until just about to boil. Add corn flour slurry, stirring until conserve is thick. Remove from heat.

- **Meringue.** Place egg whites and sugar into a glass or metal bowl and set over a pan of simmering water. Do not use boiling water or egg whites will cook. Stir mixture until sugar dissolves and mixture is warm to the touch. Using an electric mixer with a whisk attachment, whisk mixture until thick and cool. Takes about 15 minutes. The meringue should hold stiff peaks. Spoon into a piping bag fitted with a plain 1-cm (½-in) nozzle.

- **To serve.** Spoon some raspberry conserve into 4 shot glasses, then top with lemon curd until it almost reaches the rim of glass. Pipe meringue over lemon curd, then use a blowtorch to brown meringue. Decorate as desired. I used a gold leaf. Served lightly chilled.

iced espresso shots *serves 4*

Espresso coffee	400 ml (13½ fl oz), chilled
Ice cubes	10
Simple sugar syrup (page 204)	to taste, 100–200 ml (3⅓–6½ fl oz)

- Just minutes before serving, put espresso, ice and syrup in a cocktail shaker and shake well for 30 seconds to create froth. Pour immediately into shot glasses and serve with a straw.

strawberry & aniseed soup with sablé & goat's cheese ice cream *serves 4*

Sugar	95 g (3$\frac{1}{3}$ oz)
Water	50 ml (1$\frac{2}{3}$ fl oz)
Frozen strawberries	350 g (12 oz), thawed, or any fresh or frozen fruit
Fresh orange juice	100 ml (3$\frac{1}{3}$ fl oz), warmed
Aniseed or fennel seeds	2 tsp, lightly bruised
Sweet pastry (page 202)	1 quantity
Goat's cheese ice cream (page 211)	

- Place sugar and water in a saucepan over medium heat. Cook until light amber in colour. Takes about 5 minutes. Remove from heat and add thawed strawberries, stirring until well-coated. Add warmed orange juice and aniseed or fennel. Return to heat and simmer for 2–3 minutes to dissolve any remaining sugar crystals. Remove from heat and cool mixture slightly, before blending for 2–3 minutes until smooth. Strain through a fine sieve. Refrigerate until ready to serve.

- On a lightly floured work surface, roll out sweet pastry into a 0.3-cm ($\frac{1}{8}$-in) thick sheet. Cut out 6 small rectangular strips, each 8 x 1.5-cm (3 x $\frac{1}{2}$-in) and place onto a baking tray lined with non-stick baking paper. Sprinkle lightly with sugar and bake in a preheated oven set at 180°C (350°F). Bake for 10–12 minutes, until light golden brown. Leave to cool.

- **To serve.** Remove soup from refrigerator just before serving and pour into small glasses. Place a sablé biscuit over top of each glass. Using a melon ball scoop or teaspoon, scoop a small ball of goat's cheese ice cream and place on sablé biscuit. Serve immediately with lemon curd and raspberry meringue shots and iced expresso shots.

passion fruit *&* coconut chocolate truffles *makes 40–45*

These wee truffles are amazing with the combination of passion fruit and coconut. The passion fruit seeds give a crackle when the truffles are bitten into, but they can be omitted if you don't like them.

Truffles

Dark chocolate (preferably Belgian)	130 g (4¹/₂ oz)
Milk chocolate	130 g (4¹/₂ oz)
Double (heavy) cream	80 ml (2²/₃ fl oz)
Unsalted butter	20 g (²/₃ oz)
Passion fruit pulp, with seeds	50 g (1²/₃ oz)
Threaded coconut	75 g (2¹/₃ oz)

Coating

Icing (confectioner's) sugar	as needed
Quality cocoa powder	250 g (9 oz)
Dark chocolate	350 g (12 oz)

- **Truffles.** In a small bowl, break dark and milk chocolate into small pieces and set aside.

- Place cream and butter into a heavy-based saucepan and heat until 90°C (194°F) or just below boiling point. Remove saucepan from heat and add broken chocolate, passion fruit pulp and threaded coconut, stirring until chocolate is melted. Pour mixture into a medium plastic container, then leave to set for 1–2 hours in the refrigerator. Using a teaspoon, scoop out 40–45 heaped teaspoonfuls of truffle mixture. Set aside.

- **Coating.** Powder the palms of your hands with icing sugar and roll scooped out truffle mixture into even balls. Place balls onto a tray lined with non-stick baking paper. Refrigerate until firm. Takes about 1 hour.

- When truffles are almost ready, sift cocoa powder into a tray and set aside.

- Break dark chocolate for coating into a bowl and place over simmering water. Stir until chocolate is melted. Set aside to cool. When cool, cover your hands with melted dark chocolate, then pick up a chilled truffle and roll to obtain a thin, even covering of chocolate around balls. Place into sifted cocoa powder and move tray back and forth to get an even coating. Remove truffles and place on a lined tray to set. Store refrigerated until required.

- **To serve.** Remove truffles from refrigerator 30 minutes before serving.

menu two

Petite Pumpkin & Chive Baguettes

★★★

**Lime & Lemon Rice Soup with Lily Root
& Wild Fennel Pollen-dusted Frog Legs**
Wine: Sauvignon Blanc, Loire

★★★

**Duck Breast & Ravioli of Duck Leg Confit
with Orange and Cinnamon Foam**
Wine: Cabernet Sauvignon or Merlot, California

★★★

**Warm Coconut Bread Pudding with
Tropical Spiced Fruit Compote**
Wine: Beerenauslese

★★★

**Chinese Five-Spice
Chocolate Almond Macarons**

★★★

Tea & Coffee

coconut & coriander barley with lemon & honey pigeon *serves 4*

Pigeon is one of the tastiest little birds. It is not as rich as heavy game, but it is a universe away from chicken. When perfectly roasted and rested, this is a gourmet treat.

Pigeon breasts	8
Cooking oil	50 ml (1²/₃ fl oz)
Coriander leaves (cilantro) for garnish	
Salt	to taste
Ground black pepper	to taste

Coconut & coriander barley

Cooking oil	
Barley	100 g (3¹/₂ oz)
Chicken stock (page 205)	200 ml (6¹/₂ fl oz)
Coconut milk	50 ml (1²/₃ fl oz)
Butter	15 g (¹/₂ oz)
Parmesan cheese	10 g (¹/₃ oz), grated
Salt	to taste
Ground black pepper	to taste
Coriander leaves (cilantro)	20 g (²/₃ oz), chopped

Lemon & honey

White wine vinegar	300 ml (10 fl oz / 1¹/₄ cups)
Lime juice	50 ml (1²/₃ fl oz)
Honey	100 g (3¹/₂ oz)
Ground black pepper	6 g (¹/₅ oz)
Demi glace (page 206)	4 tsp

Tropical salsa

Freshly diced tomato (flesh and skin only)	100 g (3¹/₂ oz), soft centres removed
Freshly diced cucumber	100 g (3¹/₂ oz), seeds removed
Olive oil	50 ml (1²/₃ fl oz)
Lemon segments	2, roughly cut
Coriander leaves (cilantro)	50 g (1²/₃ oz)
Salt	to taste
Ground black pepper	to taste

- **Coconut & coriander barley.** In a saucepan, heat some oil and sweat barley. Gradually add chicken stock and coconut milk and continue to cook until there is just a little bite left in the grains. Stir in butter and cheese. Set aside.

- **Lemon & honey.** Place white wine vinegar in a small saucepan and reduce by half over low heat. Add lime juice, honey, pepper and demi glace and mix well. Set aside.

- **Tropical salsa.** Place all items in a mixing bowl and mix well together. Set aside until ready to serve.

- **Pigeon.** Heat oil in pan and sear pigeon breasts, skin side down first. Cook until skin is golden brown and crispy, then turn breasts over and sear on the other side. Season with salt and pepper, then deglaze pan with lemon and honey. Reserve liquid.

- **To serve.** Place a 6-cm (2¹/₂-in) square cutter on one side of a serving plate. Season coconut and coriander barley with salt and pepper, then mix in chopped coriander. Spoon mixture into cutter and allow it to sit and take the form of the mould while arranging other components of the dish. Arrange two pigeon breasts beside barley, together with some tropical salsa. Spoon some lemon and honey sauce on plate. Gently remove square cutter and garnish barley with a little more salsa and coriander. Repeat with remaining ingredients.

This is a real meeting of cultural sweet treats, and the flavours work wonderfully together. Fondant cakes are classically French, peanut butter is typically American, sesame seeds and ginger are very Asian and the ice cream compliments the dish beautifully. When you cut into the cake, the centre will ooze out with hot liquid chocolate and peanut butter sauce. A real hidden treasure in this dessert.

hot chocolate *&* peanut butter fondant cake with toasted sesame seed ginger snap *&* chocolate chip ice cream *serves 4*

Caramel sauce (page 60)
Chocolate chip ice cream
  (page 211)

Chocolate cake

72% dark chocolate (or the best you can buy)	90 g (3¹/₆ oz), chopped
Butter	90 g (3¹/₆ oz), softened + more for greasing moulds
Castor (superfine) sugar	55 g (2 oz)
Eggs	2, small
Plain (all-purpose) flour	55 g (2 oz) + more for dusting moulds
Crunchy peanut butter	4 rounded tsp

Ginger snaps

Butter	45 g (1¹/₂ oz)
Golden syrup	30 g (1 oz)
Sugar	35 g (1¹/₄ oz)
Plain (all-purpose) flour	20 g (²/₃ oz)
Ground ginger	¹/₂ tsp
White and black sesame seeds	3 tsp each, lightly toasted

- **Chocolate cake.** Start preparations a day ahead. Grease 4 cake moulds of 90-ml (3-fl oz) capacity with melted butter, then dust lightly with flour. Set aside on a baking tray. Place chocolate into a bowl set over a saucepan of simmering water. Add softened butter and stir until mixture is melted and smooth. Set aside.

- In a separate bowl with a hand whisk, beat sugar and eggs until colour begins to change. Take care not to whisk mixture too much or the cakes will collapse after baking.

- Fold chocolate and butter mixture into egg and sugar mixture and when almost fully incorporated, fold in flour until well incorporated and there is no trace of flour left.

- Pour batter evenly into prepared baking moulds and cover with plastic wrap. Refrigerate overnight.

- **Ginger snaps.** The following day, place butter, golden syrup and sugar into a bowl set over a saucepan of simmering water. Gently melt together, then remove from heat. Sift flour and ground ginger together, then mix in sesame seeds. Add to syrup and mix well.

- Drop a teaspoonful of mixture onto a baking tray lined with non-stick baking paper. Spread mixture out into a 9-cm (3½-in) round. Repeat to make another three rounds. Place tray into a preheated oven set at 180ºC (350°F) and bake for about 5 minutes. Remove from oven, allow to cool, then gently remove from tray using a spatula. Store in an airtight container until ready to assemble dessert.

- **To serve.** Remove baking moulds from refrigerator 10 minutes before you are ready to serve dessert and place into a preheated oven set at 230ºC (450°F). Bake for 7–8 minutes. The outer layer of cake should be cooked and the inside still be liquid.

- Tip hot cakes out of moulds directly onto the middle of each serving plate so cakes are upside down. Bring to the table, then place a scoop of ice cream on top of cake and garnish with a ginger snap. Finish by adding 1 Tbsp caramel sauce in a line down the side of the plate. The hot chocolate and peanut butter liquid will flow out to greet your guests when they cut into the cake.

chinese five-spice & rum snowball cookies *makes 30*

These cookies look like mini snowballs. Spices, almonds and citrus peel are packed together, submerged in a rum syrup, then rolled in a spiced icing sugar coating. Enjoy the powdery explosion of tastes as you bite into them.

Cookie dough

Butter	40 g (1¹/₂ oz), softened
Sugar	80 g (2⁴/₅ oz)
Egg	1, small
Plain (all-purpose) flour	120 g (4¹/₄ oz)
Baking powder	¹/₄ tsp
Ground cinnamon	¹/₄ tsp
Chinese five-spice powder	¹/₄ tsp
Lemon	¹/₂, grated for zest
Ground almonds	30 g (1 oz)
Candied orange peel	10 g (¹/₃ oz), finely chopped
Candied citron peel	10 g (¹/₃ oz), finely chopped

Dipping syrup

Water	150 ml (5 fl oz)
Sugar	150 g (5¹/₃ oz)
Rum	50 ml (1²/₃ fl oz)

Spiced icing sugar

Icing (confectioner's) sugar	200 g (7 oz)
Chinese five-spice powder	10 g (¹/₃ oz)

- **Cookie dough.** Place butter and sugar into a mixing bowl. Using a wooden spoon or hand-held electric beater, beat until mixture is creamy and a little fluffy. Add egg and beat to incorporate.

- Sift flour, baking powder and ground cinnamon together into a bowl. Add lemon zest, almonds, candied orange and citron peel and mix well. Add to butter, sugar and egg mixture and mix until evenly combined. Refrigerate until firm.

- Using a teaspoon, scoop up 30 small portions of cookie dough, each about 30 g (1 oz) and roll into balls with floured hands. Arrange balls 2 cm (1 in) apart on a baking tray lined with non-stick baking paper. Bake in a preheated oven set at 200°C (400°F) for about 10 minutes, or until cookies are golden brown. Remove from tray and place on a wire rack to cool.

- **Dipping syrup.** Place water and sugar into a small saucepan and bring to the boil. Remove from heat and stir in rum. Leave to cool to about 60°C (140°F) before using.

- **Spiced icing sugar.** Sift icing sugar and five-spice powder together into a bowl. Do this several times to ensure they are well mixed.

- **To serve.** Insert a long bamboo skewer into the side of each cookie. Dip cookies into 60°C (140°F) syrup for 5 seconds, then into spiced icing sugar. Serve arranged as desired. I made a special stand with little holes for the skewers so they stand upright.

Basics to Baking

Mixing or Kneading Bread Dough by Hand

Mixing or kneading should be fun and enjoyable. Ensure that you knead on a solid surface of suitable height with plenty of space. The secret to kneading is to take a 30-second to 1-minute rest every few minutes during the kneading process. This allows both you and the dough to relax.

1. Place flour in a large bowl. Sprinkle other dry ingredients around flour. Mix to combine.

2. Slowly add water and other liquids into centre of bowl of dry ingredients. Always keep a small amount of water back to adjust dough to correct consistency.

3. Using a wooden spoon or your hand, mix wet ingredients with dry ingredients in a circular motion to form a firm dough.

4. Tip dough out onto a lightly floured work surface. Have a small bowl of flour handy for dusting work surface during kneading process.

5. Push and fold dough back on itself, turning it 90° and repeating this procedure. Adjust consistency of dough by adding more flour or water if necessary. All bread recipes in this book should take in the exact amounts of liquids specified and only minor adjustments should be necessary.

6. Continue to knead dough for about 15 minutes until it is smooth and elastic. Let dough rest for 30 seconds to 1 minute after every 2–3 minutes of kneading. The dough will become smooth and elastic more quickly.

Understanding When Dough is Fully Mixed

This is the key to successful bread-making. Good bread flour contains a protein called gluten which gives structure and strength to yeast-raised goods. In order for gluten to be developed, the proteins (glutenin and gliadin) must first absorb water or other liquids. Then, as the dough is kneaded, the gluten forms elastic strands known as the gluten network which captures the gases produced by the yeast in tiny pockets or cells, causing the dough to rise and expand. If the gluten network within the dough has not been correctly developed, these gases will escape and the dough will not rise.

Main factors affecting development of dough
- Temperature of water
- Speed of kneading
- Selection and amounts of raw ingredients. High fat and sugar doughs take less time to mix due to the "shortening" and "softening" effect these ingredients have on the gluten network.

Characteristics of fully mixed dough
- A smooth and elastic texture.
- A small piece of dough can be stretched to achieve a smooth satiny sheen which is elastic and extensible. This is known as the "stretch test".

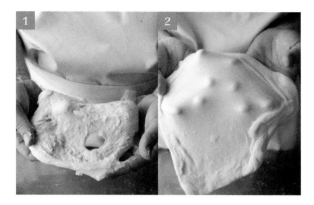

1. Underdeveloped dough has a rough texture and breaks easily when stretched out.
2. Well-developed dough is smooth, elastic and extensible when stretched.

Basic Bread-Making Terms

Bulk fermentation: Also known as first rising, this refers to the length of time that the dough is allowed to ferment in bulk. The period is measured from the end of mixing to the start of scaling, or dividing, the dough. This varies from 1 to 18 hours, depending on the levels of salt and yeast in the recipe, and the dough temperature, which should be between 25°C (77°F) and 27°C (80°F).

During bulk fermentation:
- Place dough into a lightly oiled container large enough to allow dough to double in size.
- Cover dough to prevent a skin from forming on the surface.
- Place dough in a warm place where the temperature will remain constant.

Knocking back or deflating dough: During bulk fermentation, the dough increases in volume as a result of the gases given off by the yeast. To avoid the gases escaping prematurely, the dough is gently knocked back or deflated. This is done by hand, by very gently pushing and folding the dough, three-quarters of the way through the bulk fermentation period.

Knocking back is done to:
- Expel gases and revitalise activity of the yeast.
- Even out temperature of the dough which will be warmer on the inside, and colder on the outside.
- Stimulate and help develop the gluten network.
- Even out the cell structure.

Once the knocking back stage has been completed, the dough is returned to the container and covered until it is required for scaling. In this book, the bulk fermentation and knocking back times are specified within the recipes where appropriate.

Dividing or scaling: This can be done after mixing or bulk fermentation. Using scales and a dough scraper, gently divide dough into the required sizes and weights. This should be done as quickly as possible to avoid excessive fermentation of the dough.

Rounding: After dividing or scaling, the dough pieces are shaped into smooth, round balls. This helps keep the gases within the fermenting dough. Cup your hands over the dough piece and applying a little pressure, move the dough in a circular motion, keeping it in contact with the work surface all the time. Avoid rounding on a floured surface as you want the dough to grip the work surface. This movement stretches the surface of the dough so it is completely smooth except for a seam at the bottom where the dough has gripped the work surface.

Intermediate prove: Also first prove, recovery time or bench time. This is a resting period of between 10 and 15 minutes, and takes place after rounding and before final shaping to allow the gluten network to relax. Cover the dough pieces with plastic wrap, a dough cloth or clean tea towel to avoid a skin forming on the dough surface. If insufficient intermediate prove time is given, the dough will tear and become misshapen during final shaping.

Final shaping: After intermediate prove, shape or mould the dough pieces into their final shape before placing directly into bread tins, proving baskets or onto baking trays. Correct shaping is critical to the baked loaf or roll. All shaped bread doughs have a seam which should always be placed faced down on trays and in tins to avoid splitting during the baking process. The exception is when using cane proving baskets were the smooth surface should be facing down. Once the final shaping has been done, toppings can be put onto the dough.

1. To shape a round cob or boule loaf, turn the scrunched up bottom onto the work surface, cup your hands over and move in a circular motion until a tight skin is formed.
2. To shape dough for tin bread, roll it into a tight pinwheel log, then place into tin seam side down.
3. To shape flat tray bread with pointed tapered ends, such as baguettes, use your thumb and the heel of your other hand to make a tight seal.
4. To shape dinner rolls or buns, use the palm of your hand to roll the dough on the work surface to shape them into round balls.

Final prove: Often known as proving, this is critical for product quality and should be monitored closely. Once the dough is ready to enter the prover (a piece of equipment, similar to an oven, with controlled temperature and humidity), there are three main areas to pay attention to:

1. Temperature: The ideal temperature should be between 35°C (95°F) and 40°C (104°F) to prevent the dough from chilling and to allow the yeast to function effectively.
2. Humidity: This prevents the dough from drying and forming a skin which will prevent a glossy crust forming during steaming and baking. Lack of humidity will slow proving while high humidity could cause par-baking. Spraying the dough lightly with water could help prevent skinning during proving.
3. Time: This will vary depending on dough size, final dough temperature, yeast levels and ingredients used.

If a prover is not available, come as close to the above conditions as possible by covering the dough loosely to retain moisture and setting it in a warm place.

Under-proved: When a finger is lightly pressed into the dough and the indentation springs out quickly to its original shape, more prove time is required.

Correctly proved: When a finger is lightly pressed into the dough and the indentation springs back slowly, and leaves a small indentation, the dough is correctly proved and ready to enter the oven.

Over-proved: When a finger is lightly pressed into the dough and the dough does not spring back. You should place the dough into the oven as soon as possible at the correct oven temperature, but the final product will be of poor quality.

Cutting or slashing: This is done by using a razor blade or sharp knife. Cutting should be done when the dough is three-quarters way through the prove.

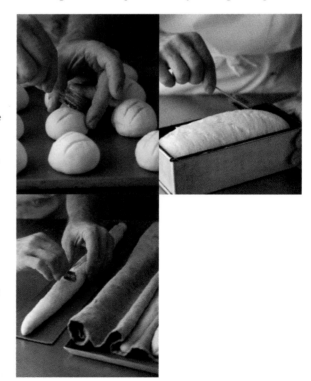

Seeding: This refers to sprinkling seeds or grated cheese over the loaf or rolls after the final shaping or just before placing the loaf or rolls into the oven. The loaf or rolls may need to be lightly sprayed with water so the seeds will stick to the surface of dough.

Dusting: This refers to dusting fully proved loaf or rolls with flour so it will bake onto the product. Dusting and cutting are usually done together to achieve a decorative pattern on the baked product.

Baking: Proved dough is fragile until the flour proteins have been coagulated (set) by baking. Handle the dough with care when loading it into the preheated oven. The yeast will lift the dough once more before it is killed by the excessive heat in the oven. This is known as oven spring. For this to take place, the condition within the oven must be hot and moist. Professional bakers use steam-injected ovens to prevent the crust from drying out and give the loaf or rolls their characteristic bloom (golden brown crust). In a domestic oven, an ovenproof dish placed on the bottom shelf of the oven with 4 to 5 cubes of ice will help create steam. Alternatively, a water spray bottle can be used to spray warm water on the baking stone of the oven 1 minute before placing the dough in to bake. Repeat this 2 to 3 times within the first 5 minutes of baking. Ensure that you only open the oven door slightly each time to avoid excessive steam and heat loss. While spraying the baking stone, avoid spraying the dough as this will result in a final product of poor quality.

Breads can be baked on baking stones, the hearth of the oven or on trays and in tins. If baking on baking stones or the hearth of the oven, place the proved dough onto a peel (a long-handled paddle-like tool) that has been well dusted with semolina or cornmeal. Slide the peel into the oven, then with a quick forward and backward jerk of the arm, slide the dough onto the baking stone or the hearth of the oven. An overturned baking tray can also be used if a peel is not available.

Baking the ideal product is dependent on dough weight, oven temperature and baking time. Here are some estimations to baking the ideal product:

Dough Weight	Oven Temperature	Baking Time
400–500 g (14^1/$_3$–1 lb 1^1/$_2$ oz)	220°C–230°C (440°F–450°F)	30–40 minutes
100–200 g (3^1/$_2$–7oz)	200°C–210°C (400°F–410°F)	12–18 minutes

Longer baking times result in:
- thicker crusts
- greater moisture loss
- darker colour of crust

Higher baking temperatures result in:
- shorter baking times
- thinner crusts
- greater risks that larger dough pieces will be under-baked and may collapse

Lower baking temperatures result in:
- longer total baking times
- thicker crusts
- greater oven spring

To test if a loaf of bread is correctly baked, tap the bottom. If it sounds hollow, the loaf is ready.

Cooling: After baking, loaves and rolls must be left to cool for the flavour and aroma to fully develop. Place baked breads directly onto a wire rack to prevent sweating after baking. Allow the bread to cool completely before slicing to ensure even slicing.

Storing: If breads are to be served within 8 hours of baking, they may be left out in the open or stored in a paper bag. Packaging breads, however, tends to cause the crust to go soft and leathery. When freezing breads, place them into plastic bags before storing. Storing bread in the refrigerator speeds up its staling process.

Basic Recipes

DOUGH, PASTES & BATTERS

Basic Levain or Sourdough Starter

This will give the bread its character and life.

Days 1 & 2: Capturing the wild yeast

Strong bread flour	400 g (14$^1/_3$ oz)
Water (25°C / 77°F)	500 ml (16 fl oz / 2 cups)

- Place flour and water in a glass bowl and mix into a smooth batter. Cover with a piece of muslin and set aside in a warm place with plenty of fresh air, but no direct sunlight. Leave for 24 hours.

- Some bubbles may appear on the surface. This is a good sign. Beat air into the mixture with a wooden spoon, then cover again with the piece of muslin and leave for another 24 hours.

Days 3 & 4: Breeding the yeast

Water (25°C / 77°F)	200 ml (6$^1/_2$ fl oz)
Strong bread flour	200 g (7 oz)

- Bubbles should be appearing on the surface, and it is time to start building on (feeding) the yeast. To do this, pour water into the bowl and break up the culture. Add flour and mix well. Cover again with muslin and let it stand in a warm place for another 24 hours. Repeat above procedure with same quantities of water and flour.

Days 5 & 6: Feeding the yeast

- As the yeast spores multiply, you will need to feed them more regularly. About 12 hours after the feed on day 4, pour off half the culture and feed the remainder with the same quantities of flour and water as above. Feed again after another 12 hours, then leave for another 12 hours. Repeat to pour off half the culture and feed twice, as with day 5.

Day 7 & beyond: Keeping the yeast alive

- You have now captured and bred a sufficient concentration of yeast, and will need to keep them alive. This is where having a levain or sourdough starter becomes a bit like owning a pet. It needs to be fed at least 3 times a day.

First feed

Strong bread flour	40 g (1$^1/_2$ oz)
Water (25°C / 77°F)	60 ml (2 fl oz / 4 Tbsp)

- You will need a starter container that has a lid with a small air hole. Measure out 100 g (3$^1/_2$ oz) starter and place into the container. Discard the rest of the starter. Feed with first feed, then leave for 8 hours to ferment.

Second feed

Strong bread flour	80 g (2$^4/_5$ oz)
Water (25°C / 77°F)	120 ml (4 fl oz / $^1/_2$ cup)

- Measure out 200 g (7 oz) starter and continue with second feed. Leave for another 8 hours to ferment.

Third feed

Strong bread flour	160 g (5$^2/_3$ oz)
Water (25°C / 77°F)	240 ml (8 fl oz / 1 cup)

- Measure out 400 g (14$^1/_3$ oz) starter and continue with third feed. Leave for another 8 hours before starting again with first feed.

- After a couple of weeks, if all has gone well, you should have a happy and healthy starter living in your home as a new member of the family. From about day 10, it will be strong enough to make bread, and its strength will increase as it matures. As the starter ages, it will develop consistency, balance and, to a certain extent, immunity from foreign invaders.

The feeding schedule

The feeding schedule can be organised to suit your day and your baking plans. I prefer to make my dough first thing in the morning, so my feeding schedule looks something like this:

8:00 am	The day before baking, first feed
8:00 pm	The day before baking, second feed
8:00 am	The following day, make dough

If you are simply maintaining the starter and not planning to make bread, throwing out some of the starter every day is quite wasteful. Once the starter is bubbling along in a healthy way (at least 2 weeks after day 1), store it in the refrigerator. Do this after the first feed, so the yeast has some food to carry it through hibernation.

In the refrigerator, most of the wild yeast will go dormant. As time goes on, though, these dormant spores will start to die off. So while the starter is in cold storage, it will still need the occasional feed. This can be done once a week, with the same amounts as for normal feeding, and discarding the excess starter as required. You will however need to use warmer water (about 35°C / 95°F). To use a starter that has gone dormant, you will need to get it back on 2 to 3 feeds a day at room temperature, at least 2 days before you bake with it again. Dormant starter cannot be used to make bread.

Feeding amounts

The amount of water and flour fed to a starter once it is healthy varies from baker to baker, but generally, the starter should be fed with half its volume of water and half its volume of flour. Example: 250 g (9 oz) healthy starter should be fed with 125 ml (4 fl oz / 1/2 cup) water and 125 g (4 1/2 oz) strong bread flour.

Little Johnny Sourdough has just been fed. After 8 hours at room temperature, he is at his full strength, healthy, strong in flavour and full of living, breathing wild yeast.

Brioche *makes 1 loaf*

Strong bread flour	250 g (9 oz)
Salt	5 g (1/6 oz)
Sugar	25 g (1 oz)
Instant active dried yeast	5 g (1/6 oz)
Eggs	4, small
Butter	125 g (4 1/2 oz), softened
Egg wash	1 egg mixed with 2 Tbsp water

• Start preparations a day ahead.

• Place flour, salt, sugar and yeast into a large mixing bowl. Add 3 eggs and mix with a wooden spoon to form dough. Tip dough out onto a lightly floured work surface and knead for about 10 minutes, with a 30-second rest every 2–3 minutes, until dough feels smooth and elastic. Add remaining egg gradually while kneading. Dough will be slimy and sticky at the start, but this will change. Continue to knead until dough is smooth and elastic.

• Gradually add softened butter in small amounts, kneading it in each time, until dough is smooth and elastic. Place dough into a lightly oiled bowl and cover with plastic wrap. Set aside in a warm, draft-free place for 1 hour until doubled in size.

• Tip dough out onto a work surface and gently deflate it by folding it onto itself 3–4 times. Return dough to lightly oiled bowl and cover again with plastic wrap. Refrigerate for 12–15 hours to firm up dough and make it easier to work with.

• The following day, remove dough from refrigerator. Roll out into a rectangular sheet, then roll up like a Swiss roll. Place into a lightly oiled bread tin and cover with plastic wrap. Leave to rise in a warm, draft-free place until almost doubled in size. Takes 2–3 hours.

• Lightly brush surface of dough with egg wash, then bake in a preheated oven set at 180°C (350°F) for 20–25 minutes, or until golden brown. Remove from oven and place on a wire rack to cool.

Basic White Bread *makes 1 loaf*

White bread flour	300 g (11 oz)
Salt	5 g (1/6 oz)
Sugar	5 g (1/6 oz)
Instant active dried yeast	1/2 tsp
Olive oil	2 tsp
Water	185 ml (6 1/4 fl oz)
Ice cubes	3–4

• Place all ingredients, except ice cubes, into a large mixing bowl and mix with a wooden spoon into dough. Tip dough out onto a lightly floured work surface and knead for 15–20 minutes, with a 30-second rest every 3–4 minutes, until dough feels smooth and elastic.

• Lightly oil a bowl large enough to allow dough to double in bulk. Place dough in bowl and cover with plastic wrap. Leave in a warm place for 1 hour. Gently knock back dough by gently folding it back onto itself, then cover again with plastic wrap and leave for another 30 minutes.

• Tip dough out onto a lightly floured work surface, then flatten and mould it into a rectangular loaf and place into an oiled 500-g (1-lb) loaf tin. Cover with plastic wrap and leave for another 1 hour.

• Using a sharp knife or razor blade, cut down the centre of loaf lengthways. Place into a preheated oven set at 200°C (400°F) with a small ovenproof dish on the bottom shelf. Quickly place ice cubes into dish, close oven and bake for 20–25 minutes. Tip bread onto a wire rack to cool.

Note: To make wholemeal bread, replace half the white bread flour with wholemeal (wholewheat) flour, and proceed as instructed in the recipe above.

Sweet Pastry

Butter	170 g (6 oz), softened
Sugar	85 g (3 oz)
Egg	1, small
Plain (all-purpose) flour	260 g (9$^1/_5$ oz)
Vanilla essence	4 drops
Lemon	$^1/_2$, grated for zest

- In a large mixing bowl, lightly beat butter and sugar with a wooden spoon until light and creamy. Add egg and mix until combined. Add flour and mix into a paste. Mix until paste just comes clean off the bowl. Be careful not to over mix or pastry will become too elastic and doughy.

- Cover with plastic wrap. Refrigerate for $^1/_2$ hour or overnight if time permits. To use, gently re-work pastry, ensuring that it remains cold and firm.

- Roll pastry out on a lightly floured surface into a 0.3-cm ($^1/_8$-in) thick sheet, or as stated in recipe.

Chocolate Sweet Pastry

- Prepare ingredients as in sweet pastry recipe above. Sift 30 g (1 oz) cocoa powder into flour and continue as instructed above.

Puff Pastry

Strong bread flour	300 g (11 oz)
Chilled butter	50 g (1$^2/_3$ oz) + 225 g (8 oz) for layering
Salt	a good pinch
Ice cold water	150 ml (5 fl oz)
Fresh lemon juice	1 tsp

- Place flour, 50 g (1$^2/_3$ oz) chilled butter and salt into a large mixing bowl. Using the tips of your fingers, roughly break up butter and rub into flour. Add ice cold water and lemon juice and mix with your hands into a firm dough.

- Tip dough out onto a lightly floured work surface and knead for 2–3 minutes. Form into a ball. Cover with plastic wrap and leave for 5–10 minutes. Using a rolling pin, roll rested dough on a lightly floured work surface into a 25-cm (10-in) square sheet, about 1-cm ($^1/_2$-in) thick.

- Ensure layering butter is the same consistency as dough. This can be done by hitting the chilled butter with a rolling pin to soften it. While doing so, shape butter into a 17-cm (7-in) square, then place it inside the square of dough.

- Fold corners of dough over butter, so they meet at the centre, resulting in 2 layers of dough and 1 layer of layering fat.

- Roll out pastry into a rectangular sheet 1-cm ($^1/_2$-in) thick. Mentally divide rectangle into thirds (see Figure 1) and fold A to C, then D to B to obtain 3 layers of pastry.

- Cover pastry with plastic wrap to prevent it from drying out and forming a skin, then let it rest for 15–20 minutes.

- Repeat to roll, fold, cover and rest pastry another 3 times. The pastry is now ready to be rolled out as required. It can be kept in the refrigerator for up to 3 days, or in the freezer until required.

Figure 1. Rolling and folding to achieve a half fold.

Short or Brisée Pastry

Plain (all-purpose) flour	240 g (5$\frac{1}{2}$ oz)
Butter	180 g (6$\frac{1}{2}$ oz)
Cold water	70 ml (2$\frac{1}{3}$ fl oz)
Salt	a good pinch

- Place flour, butter and salt into a large mixing bowl. Using fingertips, gently rub ingredients together until they resemble rough bread crumbs. Be careful not to over mix, or the butter will begin to melt from the heat of your fingers.

- Mix water into dough. Cover with plastic wrap. Refrigerate for 30 minutes or overnight.

- Before using, gently re-work pastry, taking care to ensure pastry remains cold and firm. On a lightly floured surface, roll pastry out into a 0.3-cm ($\frac{1}{8}$-in) thick sheet, or as stated in recipe.

Basic Sponge

Eggs	4
Castor (superfine) sugar	125 g (4$\frac{1}{2}$ oz)
Plain (all-purpose) flour	125 g (4$\frac{1}{2}$ oz)
Vanilla essence (optional)	a few drops
Butter	50 g (1$\frac{2}{3}$ oz), melted

- Oil and flour a 20-cm (8-in) cake tin. Preheat oven to 190°C (370°F). Break eggs into a cup and stand in a bowl of warm water. Stir with a fork to allow eggs to warm up evenly.

- Using an electric mixer with a whisk attachment, whisk together warmed eggs and sugar to ribbon stage. This refers to the stage when the mixture is thick and when trailed on itself, will hold its own weight for about 10 seconds before sinking.

- Sift flour and carefully fold through whisked eggs. Once flour is three-quarters way incorporated, add vanilla essence and melted butter and continue to fold through gently. Avoid over mixing at this stage, or you will lose the air bubbles created.

- Immediately transfer mixture to prepared cake tin and bake until sponge is set. Takes 25–30 minutes.

Pasta Dough

Italian 00 flour or plain (all-purpose) flour	550 g (19$\frac{1}{2}$ oz)
Sea salt	a pinch
Eggs	4
Egg yolks	6
Olive oil	2 Tbsp

- Put all ingredients into a blender. Blend until mixture forms coarse crumbs. Pour onto a clean, lightly floured work surface and bring together with your hands. Knead until mixture comes together as a soft, smooth dough. It should not be sticky. Cover with plastic wrap. Set aside to rest.

- Measure out the amount of dough needed and keep remaining dough wrapped in plastic.

- Flatten out dough into a 0.5-cm ($\frac{1}{4}$-in) thick sheet. If using a pasta machine, set it to the widest setting. Pass dough through the roller a few times, then reduce setting a notch and repeat to pass dough through rollers a few more times. Continue with this until you are at the thinnest setting and the dough is smooth and elastic. It is now ready to be cut, filled or shaped.

Note: 00 flour is a low-gluten flour.

SWEET SAUCES & CREAMS

Raspberry Soup or Raspberry Coulis

Fresh or frozen raspberries	220 g (8 oz)
Sugar	50 g (1$\frac{2}{3}$ oz), or to taste
Lemon juice	to taste

- Place raspberries into a saucepan and bring to the boil. Stir in sugar to dissolve. Place mixture into a blender and purée, then strain into a small bowl through a very fine sieve to remove any seeds.

- Adjust tartness by adding lemon juice to suit your taste. Leave to cool before using.

Basil Syrup

Sugar	150 g (5$\frac{1}{3}$ oz)
Water	150 ml (5 fl oz)
Basil leaves	$\frac{1}{2}$ cup
Spinach leaves	$\frac{1}{4}$ cup

- Heat sugar and water in a small saucepan. Stir until sugar is dissolved. Leave to cool before using.

- Blanch basil and spinach in a pot of boiling water for 10 seconds. Refresh in iced water immediately, then squeeze out any excess water. Chop coarsely and place in a blender with 60 ml (2 fl oz / 4 Tbsp) cooled syrup. Process for about 3 minutes to get a bright green purée. Strain through a fine sieve. Store refrigerated.

Cranberry Sauce

Red wine	100 ml (3½ fl oz)
Fresh or frozen cranberries	80 g (2⅘ oz)
Honey	1 Tbsp
Ground cloves	¼ tsp
Ground cinnamon	¼ tsp

- Place all ingredients into a saucepan and bring to the boil. Simmer for 15 minutes, then remove from heat and leave to cool. Set aside until required.

- Cranberry sauce will keep refrigerated for up to 5 days.

Creme Chantilly

Single (light) cream	200 ml (6½ fl oz)
Castor (superfine) sugar	25 g (1 oz)
Vanilla pod	1, split; seeds scraped

- Place cream, sugar and vanilla seeds into a bowl and whisk until stiff peaks form. Cover bowl and refrigerate until required.

- You may need to re-whip the cream a little before serving to achieve the required consistency.

Balsamic Reduction

Balsamic vinegar	350 ml (11⅘ fl oz)
Brown sugar	1 Tbsp
Star anise	1
Cinnamon stick	½

- Place all ingredients in a small saucepan. Simmer over low heat until only one-third of liquid remains. Takes about 1½ hours.

- Liquid should be thick and syrupy. Strain through a fine sieve. Discard star anise and cinnamon stick. Leave to cool, then pour into a squeeze bottle.

- Store and use at room temperature. Balsamic reduction keeps for a long time.

Calvados Apple Purée

Granny Smith apples	2
Water	50 ml (1⅔ fl oz)
Calvados liquor	100 ml (3⅓ fl oz)

- Peel, core and cube apples. Place into a small saucepan with water, cover with a lid and bring to the boil. Reduce heat to a simmer and cook until apples are completely soft, stirring occasionally to avoid apples colouring and burning.

- Add liquor and cook for another 2 minutes. Remove from heat and purée using a hand-held blender until smooth. Pass purée through a fine sieve to remove any lumps. Leave to cool before using. Cover and keep refrigerated for up to 2 days.

Apricot Glaze

Apricot jam	300 g (11 oz)
Water	150 ml (5 fl oz)

- Place apricot jam and water in a saucepan and stir to mix. Bring to the boil and remove from heat. Pass mixture through a sieve to remove any lumps and use while still hot. You may need to warm the glaze from time to time. This can be done using the microwave oven.

Simple Sugar Syrup

Sugar	200 g (7 oz)
Water	200 ml (6½ fl oz)

- Place sugar and water into a small saucepan and bring to the boil, stirring to dissolve sugar. Remove from heat and leave to cool.

- Store refrigerated in an airtight container.

SAVOURY SAUCES & STOCKS

Pesto Sauce

Basil	100 g (3½ oz)
Pine nuts	15 g (½ oz), toasted
Parmesan cheese	25 g (1 oz), grated
Extra virgin olive oil	75 ml (2½ fl oz)
Salt	to taste
Ground black pepper	to taste

- Wash and pick through basil to remove any stems or bruised leaves. Place in a blender with pine nuts, Parmesan and a little olive oil. Purée.

- With motor running, add remaining olive oil in a steady stream until sauce reaches desired consistency. Season to taste with salt and pepper.

Aioli *Makes 200 ml (6½ fl oz)*

Egg yolk	1
Dijon mustard	8 g (¼ oz)
Lemon juice	4 tsp
Garlic	10 g (⅓ oz), peeled and minced
Sunflower seed oil	200 ml (6½ fl oz)
Salt	to taste
Ground black pepper	to taste

- Place egg yolk, mustard, lemon juice and garlic in a blender and process. With motor running, add oil in a slow, steady stream.

- Adjust consistency with a little warm water if mixture becomes too thick. Season to taste with salt and pepper.

Mayonnaise

Egg yolks	2
White wine vinegar	1 tsp
Sea salt	a good pinch
Dijon mustard	1 tsp
Light olive oil	300 ml (10 fl oz / 1¼ cups)

- Put egg yolks, vinegar, salt and mustard into a blender and mix until creamy. With motor running, add olive oil gradually until well incorporated and mixture is emulsified. Adjust seasoning to taste.

- If mayonnaise splits, fix it by mixing in a separate bowl, 1 egg yolk, a pinch of salt and a small teaspoon of mustard, then adding it to the mixture in the blender.

Chicken Stock *makes 1 litre (32 fl oz / 4 cups)*

Chicken bones	500 g (1 lb 1½ oz), washed in cold water
Celery	100 g (3½ oz), roughly cut
Carrots	75 g (2⅓ oz), roughly cut
Onions	150 g (5⅓ oz), roughly cut
Bay leaves	15 g (½ oz)
Water	1.5 litres (48 fl oz / 6 cups)
White peppercorns	2 g (1/15 oz)
Parsley	5 g (1/6 oz)
Rosemary	2 g (1/15 oz)

- Put all ingredients into a pot and fill with cold water. Bring slowly to the boil, then simmer over low heat for 1½ hours. Turn off heat and let rest for 1 hour. Strain before using.

- Chicken stock will keep refrigerated for up to 5 days, or frozen for up to 1 month.

Court Bouillon *makes 2.5 litres (80 fl oz / 10 cups)*

Carrots	100 g (3½ oz), roughly cut
Onion	150 g (5⅓ oz), roughly cut
Celery	100 g (3½ oz), roughly cut
Leek	100 g (3½ oz), roughly cut
Fennel trimmings	150 g (5⅓ oz)
Salt	25 g (1 oz)
Black peppercorns	10 g (⅓ oz)
Bay leaves	5 g (1/6 oz)
Caraway seeds	8 g (¼ oz)
Water	2.5 litres (80 fl oz / 10 cups)

- Put all ingredients into a pot and bring to the boil. Boil for a few minutes, then remove from heat. Strain before using.

- Court bouillon will keep refrigerated for up to 5 days, or frozen for up to 1 month.

Giblet Gravy

Turkey bones	1 kg (2 lb 3 oz)
Olive oil	50 ml (1⅔ fl oz)
Onion	1, large, peeled and diced
Celery	3 sticks, diced
Carrot	1, diced
Tomato paste	30 g (1 oz)
White wine	200 ml (6½ fl oz)
Cold water	2.5 litres (80 fl oz / 10 cups)
Thyme	1 sprig, finely chopped
Rosemary	1 sprig, finely chopped
Sage	4-5 leaves, finely chopped
Salt	to taste
Ground black pepper	to taste
Giblets	200 g (7 oz)
Unsalted butter	50 g (1⅔ oz)

- Place turkey bones on a baking tray and roast in the oven at 200°C (400°F) for 1 hour, or until dark brown. Remove from oven.

- Heat oil in a deep saucepan and cook onion, celery and carrot until caramelised and slightly soft. Add tomato paste and cook for 2 minutes.

- Add roasted turkey bones and deglaze with white wine. Reduce wine by half, then add cold water. Slowly bring to a boil and use a ladle to skim off any impurities on the surface.

- Add herbs to infuse, then strain liquid into a small saucepan and place over low heat. Reduce, uncovered, to about 200 ml (6½ fl oz). Taste and adjust with salt and pepper.

- Parboil giblets in a pot of boiling water and dice. Add to gravy and bring to the boil. Reduce heat and simmer for 30 minutes. Use as needed.

Demi Glace *makes 250 ml (8 fl oz / 1 cup)*

Beef bones	2 kg (4 lb 6 oz)
Olive oil	5 tsp
White onions	700 g (1¹/₂ lb), peeled and cut into medium dice
Celery	300 g (11 oz), cut into medium dice
Carrots	400 g (14¹/₃ oz), cut into medium dice
Tomato paste	100 g (3¹/₂ oz)
Pig's trotters	200 g (7 oz)
Red wine	400 ml (13¹/₂ fl oz)
Cold water	5 litres (160 fl oz / 20 cups)
Bay leaves	2 g (¹/₁₅ oz)
Juniper berries	2 g (¹/₁₅ oz)
Thyme	5 g (¹/₆ oz)
Rosemary	3 g (¹/₁₀ oz)
Parsley	10 g (¹/₃ oz)
Black peppercorns	5 g (¹/₆ oz)

- Place beef bones on a baking tray and roast in the oven at 200°C (400°F) for 1 hour, or until dark brown.

- Heat oil in a large pot and roast onion, celery and carrots until caramelised and slightly soft. Add tomato paste and cook for 2 minutes.

- Add beef bones and pig's trotters, then deglaze with red wine. Reduce by half, then add cold water. Slowly bring to the boil and use a ladle to skim off any impurities on the surface.

- Boil for at least 6 hours. During the last hour of cooking, add remaining ingredients to infuse, then strain into a smaller pot.

- Reduce to 250 ml (8 fl oz / 1 cup) and adjust seasoning to taste. Use as needed.

Vinaigrette

Extra virgin olive oil	100 ml (3¹/₂ fl oz)
Red wine vinegar	2 Tbsp
Salt	to taste
Ground black pepper	to taste

- Combine ingredients in a bottle or screw-top jar. Use as needed.

- Adjust flavour and taste of dressing by using peanut oil or different types of vinegars as desired. You can also add 1 tsp mustard or honey for a fuller flavour.

Tomato Ragout *makes 500 ml (16 fl oz / 2 cups)*

Tomatoes	750 g (1 lb 10¹/₂ oz)
Tomato paste	25 g (1 oz)
Olive oil	40 ml (1¹/₃ fl oz)
Onion	1, small, peeled and finely diced
Garlic	50 g (1²/₃ oz), peeled and finely sliced
Salt	to taste
Ground black pepper	
Oregano	10 g (¹/₃ oz)
Basil leaves	10 g (¹/₃ oz), julienne

- Using a small knife, cut stems from top of tomatoes, then score an 'X' in the skin at the bottom of each tomato.

- Place into a pot of boiling water for 1 minute, then remove. When cool enough to handle, peel and discard skin. Cut tomatoes into quarters and spoon out seeds.

- Blend seeds with tomato paste, then pass through a sieve to get purée. Dice tomato flesh.

- Heat oil in a frying pan and sweat onion and garlic. Add diced tomato and tomato purée. Season to taste with salt and pepper, then cover with a lid and slowly simmer for 5 minutes. Add oregano leaves and simmer for another 5 minutes. Add basil just before serving. Use as needed.

PURÉES & FOAMS

Lemon Foam

Cooking oil	2 tsp
Onion	¹/₂, peeled and sliced
Garlic	10 g (¹/₃ oz), peeled and sliced
White wine	2 tsp
Chicken stock (page 205)	300 ml (10 fl oz / 1¹/₄ cups)
Lemons	2, juice extracted
Butter	10 g (¹/₃ oz)
Soy lecithin	2 g (¹/₁₅ oz)
Salt	to taste

- Heat oil in a saucepan and sweat onion and garlic. Deglaze with white wine, then add chicken stock and bring to the boil. Lower heat and simmer for 15 minutes.

- Pass mixture through a chinoise and return liquid to the pot. Reheat and stir in lemon juice, butter, soy lecithin and salt. Create foam from mixture using a hand-held blender when ready to serve.

Coconut Foam

Cooking oil	
Shallots	50 g (1²/₃ oz), peeled and finely chopped
Garlic	5 g (¹/₆ oz), peeled and finely sliced
Chicken stock (page 205)	500 ml (16 fl oz / 2 cups)
Coriander leaves (cilantro)	50 g (1²/₃ oz), sliced
Kaffir lime leaves	3 g (¹/₁₀ oz), sliced
Ginger	20 g (²/₃ oz), peeled and cut into fine strips
Coconut milk	200 ml (6½ fl oz)
Fish sauce	to taste
Lime juice	4 tsp

- Heat oil in a saucepan and sweat shallots and garlic. Add chicken stock and bring to the boil. Add coriander, lime leaves and ginger. Return to the boil, then lower heat and simmer to infuse flavours.

- Strain liquid back into pan. Stir in coconut milk and add fish sauce to taste. Return to the boil, then set aside. Create foam from mixture using a hand-held blender when ready to serve.

White Tomato Foam

Cherry tomatoes	500 g (1 lb 1½ oz)
Butter	20 g (²/₃ oz), softened
Soy lecithin	1 g (¹/₃₀ oz)
Salt	to taste

- Purée tomatoes. Line a sieve with clean muslin cloth and set over a bowl. Pour tomato purée into sieve and leave to drain overnight.

- The following day, place tomato juice in a pan over low heat. Whisk in butter and soy lecithin. Season with salt. Create foam from mixture using a hand-held blender when ready to serve.

Orange & Cinnamon Foam

Cooking oil	2 tsp
Onion	100 g (3½ oz), peeled and sliced
Garlic	10 g (¹/₃ oz), peeled and sliced
White wine	2 tsp
Chicken stock (page 205)	200 ml (6½ fl oz)
Orange juice	200 ml (6½ fl oz)
Cinnamon stick	1 g (¹/₃₀ oz), grated
Salt	to taste
Butter	10 g (¹/₃ oz)
Soy lecithin	2 g (¹/₁₅ oz)

- Heat oil in a saucepan and sweat onion and garlic. Deglaze with white wine, then add chicken stock, orange juice and cinnamon stick. Bring to the boil, then lower heat and simmer for 15 minutes.

- Pass mixture through a chinoise and return liquid to the pan. Season with salt. Reheat on very low heat and add butter and soy lecithin. Create foam from mixture using a hand-held blender when ready to serve.

Cucumber & Yellow Capsicum Foam

Cucumber juice	100 ml (3¹/₃ fl oz)
Yellow capsicum (bell pepper) juice	150 ml (5 fl oz)
Olive oil	2 tsp
Onion	50 g (1²/₃ oz), peeled and chopped
Garlic	5 g (¹/₆ oz), peeled and chopped
Chicken stock (page 205)	100 ml (3¹/₃ fl oz)
Soy lecithin	1 g (¹/₃₀ oz)
Butter	10 g (¹/₃ oz)

- Extract juice from cucumbers and yellow capsicums using a juice extractor.

- Heat oil in a saucepan and sweat onion and garlic. Deglaze with chicken stock, then boil until onion is soft. Add cucumber and capsicum juices, and bring to the boil. Pass mixture through a sieve.

- Stir in soy lecithin and butter. Mix well. Create foam from mixture using a hand-held blender when ready to serve.

Pink Vinegar Foam

Onion	50 g (1²/₃ oz), peeled and chopped
Garlic	10 g (¹/₃ oz), peeled and chopped
Chicken stock (page 205)	150 ml (5 fl oz)
Chinese pink vinegar	100 ml (3¹/₃ fl oz)
Butter	25 g (1 oz), cut into cubes
Soy lecithin	2 g (¹/₁₅ oz)

- Heat oil in a saucepan and sweat onion and garlic. Add chicken stock and pink vinegar and bring to a boil. Strain and return liquid to pan. Reheat on a very low heat. Add butter and soy lecithin. Create foam from mixture using a hand-held blender when ready to serve.

Porcini Mushroom Foam

Olive oil	2 tsp
Onion	50 g (1²/₃ oz), peeled and chopped
Dried porcini mushrooms	30 g (1 oz), soaked to soften
White wine	2 tsp
Chicken stock (page 205)	1 litre (32 fl oz / 4 cups)
Salt	to taste
Ground black pepper	to taste
Soy lecithin	1.5 g (¹/₁₅ oz)

- Heat oil in a pan. Sweat onion and porcini until soft. Deglaze with white wine, then add stock. Season with salt and pepper, then pass through a fine mesh sieve. Stir in soy lecithin. Create foam from mixture using a hand-held blender when ready to serve.

Strawberry Foam

Rhubarb	250 g (9 oz), cubed
Castor (superfine) sugar	65 g (2¹/₃ oz)
White wine	6¹/₂ tsp
Cinnamon sticks	2
Gelatine leaves	4 sheets
Strawberry purée (page 209)	40 g (1¹/₂ oz)
Champagne	60 ml (2 fl oz / 4 Tbsp)

- Place rhubarb, sugar, wine and cinnamon sticks in a pot and bring to the boil. Boil until rhubarb is soft and juices are released. Remove from heat.
- Soak gelatine in a bowl of water to soften. When soft, remove and squeeze out excess water, then stir into rhubarb syrup to dissolve. Strain juice and measure out 90 ml (3 fl oz / 6 Tbsp).
- Stir strawberry purée and champagne into rhubarb syrup. Pour mixture into a cream whipper to discharge foam. Use as needed.

Aubergine Purée

Aubergines	4, large
Vegetable oil	1 Tbsp
Extra virgin olive oil	200 ml (6¹/₂ fl oz)
Thyme	1 sprig, leaves plucked, stem discarded
Black sesame paste	2 tsp
Garlic	2 cloves, peeled and crushed
Salt	to taste
Ground black pepper	to taste

- Preheat oven to 200°C (400°F).
- Wash and dry aubergines. Lay them out on a baking tray and brush skins with oil. Place into oven and roast until skins are brown. Takes at least 20 minutes. Aubergines are ready when the skins can be easily peeled off. Remove from oven and hold aubergines over a bowl to catch the juice while peeling them. Discard skins.
- Place flesh into a blender and purée with a little olive oil. Add thyme leaves, sesame paste, garlic, salt and pepper. With motor running, pour in remaining olive oil and juice. Purée should be smooth and thick.
- Season to taste, then pass mixture through a fine mesh sieve. Store refrigerated.

Fennel Purée

Butter	50 g ($1^2/_3$ oz)
Fennel	250 g (9 oz), diced
Pastis liqueur (Pernod)	50 ml ($1^2/_3$ fl oz)
Chicken stock (page 205)	100ml ($3^1/_3$ fl oz)

• Heat butter in a small saucepan and sweat fennel. Deglaze with liqueur, then add chicken stock and simmer until fennel is very soft.

• Blend mixture until very fine and smooth, then pass it through a fine mesh sieve. Use as needed.

Parsley Purée

Parsnip	500 g (1 lb $1^1/_2$ oz), peeled and diced
Vermouth	100 ml ($3^1/_3$ fl oz)
Chicken stock (page 205)	300 ml (10 fl oz / $1^1/_4$ cups)
Single (light) cream	200 ml ($6^1/_2$ fl oz)
Parsley	500 g (1 lb $1^1/_2$ oz)
Salt	to taste

• In a saucepan, cook parsnip in vermouth and chicken stock until soft and liquid has evaporated. Add cream and boil for a few more minutes. Remove from heat and blend with a hand-held blender until very fine and smooth.

• Cook parsley in a small pot of salted water until soft. Drain, then blend into a fine purée. Mix with parsnip purée. Season to taste. Use as needed.

Strawberry Purée

Fresh or frozen strawberries	100 g ($3^1/_2$ oz)
Icing (confectioner's) sugar	25 g (1 oz)

• Place strawberries and sugar into a bowl and purée with a hand-held blender. Pass through a sieve.

• Store in the refrigerator or freezer until needed.

Dill & Honey Mustard Dressing

Mayonnaise (page 205)	70 ml ($2^1/_3$ fl oz)
Honey	2 tsp
Dijon mustard	2 tsp
Pommery mustard	2 tsp
Dill	10 g ($1/_3$ oz), finely chopped
Salt	to taste
Ground black pepper	to taste

• Combine all ingredients and mix well. Adjust seasoning to taste. Use as needed.

DIPS & OTHER RECIPES

Croutons for Caesar Salad

Day-old white bread	$1/_4$ loaf
Clarified butter	as needed
Salt	to taste
Ground black pepper	to taste

• Slice bread into 1-cm ($1/_2$-in) thick slices. Remove crusts and discard, then cut bread into cubes.

• Heat some clarified butter in a pan and fry bread cubes until golden. Remove and drain on kitchen paper. Season with salt and pepper.

Croutons for Goat's Cheese Salad

• Crouton for goat's cheese salad can be made from thinly sliced baguettes brushed with light olive oil, sprinkled with salt and pepper, then grilled until golden and crisp.

Aubergine Dip *makes about 2 cups*

Aubergines (eggplants)	1, large, or 2, medium
Garlic	2 cloves, peeled and crushed
Tahini (sesame paste)	2 Tbsp
Finely chopped spring onions (scallions)	$1/_4$ cup
Lemon	1, juice extracted
Chopped parsley	$1/_4$ cup
Ground paprika	

• Preheat oven to 200°C (400°F). Prick aubergines all over with a fork. Place on a baking tray and bake for 45–50 minutes until very soft. Remove from oven and leave to cool. If pressed for time, plunge aubergines) into iced water to cool. Drain well.

• Peel and chop aubergines, then place in a blender with garlic, tahini, spring onions, lemon juice and parsley. Blend until almost smooth. Spoon into small bowls and refrigerate until ready to use. Sprinkle with paprika before using.

Olive Tapenade

Kalamata black olives	200 g (7 oz), pitted and drained
Canned tuna in oil	125 g (4½ oz), drained
Basil	20 g (⅔ oz)
Anchovy fillets in oil	4, drained
Garlic	1 clove, peeled and crushed
Lemon	1, grated for zest
Lemon juice	2 Tbsp
Extra virgin olive oil	2 Tbsp
Ground black pepper	to taste
Salt	a good pinch

- Place all ingredients except olive oil, salt and pepper in a blender. Process into a smooth and fine paste. With motor running, gradually add olive oil until smooth and well combined. Season with salt and pepper.

- This recipe makes enough for 2 batches and can be kept for up to 2 weeks.

Brandade Dip

Cod fillets	150 g (5⅓ oz), skin and bones removed
Rock salt	200 g (7 oz)
Potato	1, small
Milk	200 ml (6½ fl oz)
Thyme	1 sprig
Garlic	2 cloves, peeled
Olive oil	4 tsp
Salt	to taste
Freshly ground black pepper	to taste

- Start preparations a day ahead. Coat both sides of fillets with rock salt, then cover and leave overnight in the refrigerator. The following day, remove cod from refrigerator, rinse with cold water, then soak in cold water for 8–12 hours to fully remove salt.

- The following day, peel and dice potato, then place into a saucepan with milk, thyme and garlic. Bring to the boil and add drained cod fillets. When potato and cod are cooked, remove thyme, then place cod, potato and garlic in a blender and process to a smooth purée.

- Slowly add milk until mixture just holds its shape. The mixture will thicken slightly when left to stand. Add olive oil and blend in, then season with salt and pepper to taste. Spoon into serving bowls, cover and refrigerate until required.

Coconut Rice *serves 4*

Thai jasmine rice	2 cups
Coconut milk	500 ml (16 fl oz / 2 cups)
Water	435 ml (14 fl oz / 1½ cups)
Salt	¾ tsp
Brown sugar (optional)	1 tsp
Coconut flavouring (optional)	1 tsp
Vegetable oil	½ tsp

- You will need a deep pot with a tight-fitting lid for this dish. Oil base of pot, then add rice, coconut milk, water and salt to pot. Place over medium-high heat. Stir well.

- Add sugar and flavouring, if using. Stir occasionally to prevent rice from sticking to base of pot. Cook until coconut milk and water come to a gentle boil. Once mixture starts to bubble, stop stirring. Turn down heat to medium-low, then place lid askew on pot, so it is about three-quarters covered. Allow rice to cook for 15–20 minutes, or until rice has absorbed most of the liquid.

- Turn off heat, but leave pot on burner. Place lid on tightly and allow to sit for 5–10 minutes, or until ready to serve. The rice will "steam" and have a slightly sticky texture.

Tomato Confit

Cherry tomatoes	500 b (1 lb 1½ oz), washed, cut in half
Garlic	15 g (½ oz), peeled and thinly sliced
Salt	to taste
Ground black pepper	to taste
Thyme	1 sprig, leaves only, chopped
Virgin olive oil	40 ml (1⅓ fl oz)
Icing (confectioner's) sugar	25 g (1 oz)

- Lay tomato halves cut-side up on a baking tray. Top with garlic and season lightly with salt and pepper.

- Sprinkle chopped thyme over, then drizzle with olive oil and dust with icing sugar.

- Place tomatoes in a preheated oven set at 82°C (180°F) for 2–4 hours until tomatoes are tender and almost dry. The baking time will depend on the size of the tomatoes used.

- Leave tomato confit to cool. Use as needed, or place in an airtight jar and cover with olive oil. Store refrigerated for up to 2 weeks.

ICE CREAM & SUGAR CREATIONS

Vanilla Ice Cream

Double (heavy) cream	250 ml (8 fl oz / 1 cup)
Milk	60 ml (2 fl oz / 4 Tbsp)
Vanilla pod	1, split and seeds scraped
Egg yolks	2
Sugar	1/3 cup
Liquid glucose	1 Tbsp

- Place cream, milk and vanilla pod and seeds in a saucepan and bring to the boil. Remove from heat and set aside.

- In a bowl, whisk together egg yolks and sugar, then ladle in some hot cream and whisk again. Add mixture to rest of hot cream and stir over low heat for 2–3 minutes until mixture thickens slightly. Mixture should be smooth and coat the back of a spoon.

- Stir in glucose and remove vanilla pod. Strain through a fine mesh sieve and set aside to cool.

- Churn using an ice cream maker according to manufacturer's instructions. Freeze and use as needed.

Chocolate Chip Ice Cream

- Prepare vanilla ice cream as directed in recipe above. Add 250 g (9 oz) finely chopped chocolate when churning in ice cream maker.

Goat's Cheese Ice Cream

Double (heavy) cream	250 ml (8 fl oz / 1 cup)
Milk	60 ml (2 fl oz / 4 Tbsp)
Egg yolks	2
Sugar	1/3 cup
Goat's cheese	55 g (2 oz)
Liquid glucose	1 Tbsp

- Place cream and milk in a saucepan and bring to the boil. Remove from heat and set aside.

- In a bowl, whisk together egg yolks and sugar, then ladle in some hot cream and whisk again. Add mixture to the rest of the hot cream and stir over low heat for 2–3 minutes until mixture thickens slightly. Mixture should be smooth and coat the back of a spoon.

- Mix goat's cheese and glucose together, then add to cream mixture, stirring until smooth. Pass through a fine mesh sieve and set aside to cool.

- Churn using an ice cream maker according to manufacturer's instructions. Freeze and use as needed.

Sugar Decorations

Cold water	300 ml (10 fl oz / 1 1/4 cups)
Granulated sugar	400 g (14 1/3 oz)

- Place water and sugar in a heavy-based saucepan. Bring to the boil. Use a clean pastry brush to brush off any sugar crystals that catch on sides of pan.

- Once syrup reaches a dark amber colour, at about 150°C–160°C (300°F–325°F), remove from heat and plunge pan into a bowl of iced water to stop the cooking process. When syrup starts to thicken slightly, use immediately. If it hardens too much, place over low heat to soften again.

Caramel Cages

- Boil sugar with water in a saucepan to 150°C–160°C (300°F–350°F), then plunge immediately into a bowl of iced water. Remove and leave for 2–3 minutes until syrup starts to thicken. Lightly oil the back of a ladle.

- Dip a dessertspoon into the hot syrup and make a lattice pattern on the upturned, oiled ladle.

- Allow to cool, then snip off any stringy bits with a pair of kitchen scissors. Carefully lift cage off ladle. Set aside on non-stick baking paper until required.

Recipes

Breads

Bagel Crisps & Grissini with Aubergine & Brandade Dips & Olive Tapenade 186

Bread Cases with Olive Tapenade & Oven-roasted Tomato with Crisp Green Salad 127

Bruschetta Plate 19

    Salami & Arugula with Lemon Dressing 19

    Spiced Fig Marmalade & Blue Cheese 19

    Vine-ripened Tomato & Basil 19

Caramelised Garlic, Cherry Tomato & Rosemary Focaccia 102

Chocolate, Pecan & Cranberry Sourdough 43

Cracker & Nut Platter 66

Cheese & Walnut Crackers 66

    Sesame Seed Grissini 67

    Spiced Cocktail Nuts 67

Korean Corn & Chilli Bread 91

Mini Chinese Flower Steamed Buns with Chilli & Chives 31

Mini Wholemeal Soda Bread Sandwiches with Onion Marmalade & Dill Mayonnaise 138

Petite Garlic & Coriander Naan 55

Petite Pumpkin & Chive Baguettes 175

Smoked Paprika & Sunflower Dinner Rolls with Antipasto 150

Sun-dried Tomato Ciabatta with Extra Virgin Olive Oil & Balsamic Vinegar 114

Warmed Feta, Caramelised Garlic, Tomato & Basil Rolls 162

Whipped Brie de Meaux & Crouton Mille-Feuille with Balsamic Glaze & Arugula Salad 79

Desserts

Almond & Walnut Tartlet with Toffee Sauce & Chocolate Chip Ice Cream 120

Apple & Fennel Tarte Tatin with Vanilla Ice Cream, Calvados Apple Purée & White Chocolate Tuile 72

Carrot Cake with Cream Cheese Icing, Sweet Basil Dressing & Caramelised Poached Baby Carrots with Orange & Lemon Candied Peel 156

Chocolate & Blue Cheese Tortellini with Vanilla Ice Cream, Crunchy Praline & Caramel Sauce 60

Chocolate & Raspberry Rice Pudding with Baileys Crème Ganache 84

Espresso Crème Brûlée with Espresso Foam 96

Gluten-free Sweet Basil, Almond Citrus Cake with Orange Compote, Raspberry Soup & Natural Mango Yoghurt Fool 144

Hot Chocolate & Peanut Butter Fondant Cake with Toasted Sesame Seed Ginger Snap & Chocolate Chip Ice Cream 192

Lemon Crème Mille-Feuille with Berry Compote, Aged Balsamic Reduction, Basil Syrup & Gin Jelly Cubes 108

Raspberry Macaron Tart with Raspberry Cream, Blueberry Compote & Red Currants 48

Rosé Wine Jelly with Summer Berries 132

Sour Cherry & Cranberry Trifle 24

Sweet Potato & Chinese Wolfberry Crème Brûlée with Lavender Tuile Springs 36

Trio Dessert Tasting Plate 168

    Iced Espresso Shots 168

    Lemon Curd & Raspberry Meringue Shots 168

    Strawberry & Aniseed Soup with Sablé & Goat's Cheese Ice Cream 169

Warm Coconut Bread Pudding with Tropical Spiced Fruit Compote 180

Main Courses

Beef Rendang Curry with Braised Cabbage & Coconut Foam 166

Beef Tenderloin with Pancetta, Foie Gras Terrine, Porcini Mushrooms & French Beans 46

Char-grilled Atlantic Salmon with Baby Spring Vegetables & Salsa Verde 82

Coconut & Coriander Barley with Lemon & Honey Pigeon 190

Couscous Baked in Aubergines with Tomato & Oregano 143

Duck Breast & Ravioli of Duck Leg Confit with Orange and Cinnamon Foam 178

Fillet of Veal with Herb and Parmesan Crust, Confit Potatoes & Bone Marrow Sauce 70

Grilled Portobello Mushrooms Layered with Fennel Pollen Polenta & Aubergine Purée with Cucumber & Yellow Capsicum Foam 130

Halibut & Miso Tomato Broth with Water Spinach 107

Lobster Cannelloni with Seared Snapper, Parsley Purée & White Tomato Foam 118

Lobster, Mussel & Cod Pot-Au-Feu with Lemon Grass, Saffron and Tomato Jus 94

Pappardelle with Char-grilled Aubergine, Courgette & Capsicum on Tomato & Basil Ragout 155

Poached Mandarin Fish & Kai Lan with Chinese Rice Noodles 35

Risotto of Porcini Mushroom, Chicken Breast & Mascarpone with Crispy Skin & Lemon Foam 58

Roasted Turkey Breast with Brioche Stuffing, French Beans, Cranberry & Giblet Gravy 22

Petits Fours

Almond & Rosemary Biscotti 135

Baileys Walnut Chocolate Truffles 27

Belgium Biscuit Bites 74

Chinese Five-spice & Rum Snowball Cookies 195

Chinese Five-spice Chocolate Almond Macarons 183

Chocolate & Nut Panforte 147

Chocolate Fruit & Nut Drops 26

Citron & Raspberry Macarons 123

Starters

Basic Recipes

Weights & Measures

Quantities for this book are given in Metric and American (spoon and cup) measures. Standard spoon and cup measurements used are: 1 teaspoon = 5 ml, 1 tablespoon = 15 ml, 1 cup = 250 ml. All measures are level unless otherwise stated.

LIQUID & VOLUME MEASURES

Metric	Imperial	American
5 ml	1/6 fl oz	1 teaspoon
10 ml	1/3 fl oz	1 dessertspoon
15 ml	1/2 fl oz	1 tablespoon
60 ml	2 fl oz	1/4 cup (4 tablespoons)
85 ml	2 1/2 fl oz	1/3 cup
90 ml	3 fl oz	3/8 cup (6 tablespoons)
125 ml	4 fl oz	1/2 cup
180 ml	6 fl oz	3/4 cup
250 ml	8 fl oz	1 cup
300 ml	10 fl oz (1/2 pint)	1 1/4 cups
375 ml	12 fl oz	1 1/2 cups
435 ml	14 fl oz	1 3/4 cups
500 ml	16 fl oz	2 cups
625 ml	20 fl oz (1 pint)	2 1/2 cups
750 ml	24 fl oz (1 1/5 pints)	3 cups
1 litre	32 fl oz (1 3/5 pints)	4 cups
1.25 litres	40 fl oz (2 pints)	5 cups
1.5 litres	48 fl oz (2 2/5 pints)	6 cups
2.5 litres	80 fl oz (4 pints)	10 cups

OVEN TEMPERATURE

	°C	°F	Gas Regulo
Very slow	120	250	1
Slow	150	300	2
Moderately slow	160	325	3
Moderate	180	350	4
Moderately hot	190/200	370/400	5/6
Hot	210/220	410/440	6/7
Very hot	230	450	8
Super hot	250/290	475/550	9/10

DRY MEASURES

Metric	Imperial
30 grams	1 ounce
45 grams	1 1/2 ounces
55 grams	2 ounces
70 grams	2 1/2 ounces
85 grams	3 ounces
100 grams	3 1/2 ounces
110 grams	4 ounces
125 grams	4 1/2 ounces
140 grams	5 ounces
280 grams	10 ounces
450 grams	16 ounces (1 pound)
500 grams	1 pound, 1 1/2 ounces
700 grams	1 1/2 pounds
800 grams	1 3/4 pounds
1 kilogram	2 pounds, 3 ounces
1.5 kilograms	3 pounds, 4 1/2 ounces
2 kilograms	4 pounds, 6 ounces

LENGTH

Metric	Imperial
0.5 cm	1/4 inch
1 cm	1/2 inch
1.5 cm	3/4 inch
2.5 cm	1 inch

about the Authors

David Laris is a chef and restaurateur. He is the founder of David Laris Creates (DLC), a food and beverage consultancy and the creator of Laris, an award-winning contemporary fine dining restaurant located at the prestigious Three on the Bund in Shanghai, China.

Before his move to Shanghai, David headed Mezzo, Terence Conran's flagship restaurant in Soho, London, where he earned the restaurant countless accolades for innovative and exciting dining.

Today, David continues to create exciting contemporary fine dining concepts with influences from all over the world.

Visit www.davidlariscreates.com to learn more.

Dean Brettschenider is a professional baker and pâtissier.
A New Zealander, Dean completed his apprenticeship in his home country before venturing out to work in the US, Britain and Europe gaining experience in all areas of the trade. This includes working in top bakeries, exclusive hotels and fine dining restaurants, alongside some of Europe's leading bakers and pastry chefs.

Today, Dean is based in Shanghai, making his baked products available at David Laris Slice Delicatessen under his Baker — Dean Brettschneider brand.

Dean is the author of four other award-winning cookbooks, all produced based on his simple philosophy of commitment, dedication and passion, injected with a little fun.

Visit www.deanbrettschneider.com to learn more.

about the Photographer

Aaron McLean hails from Queenstown, New Zealand. After a decade working in restaurants around the world, he decided make a career change to become a food photographer. Today, Aaron is one of the most sought-after food and lifestyle photographers in New Zealand.

Visit www.aaronmclean.com to learn more.

With *The Menu*, David and Dean offer the aspiring cook an innovative way to put together many different recipes to create exciting menus whatever the occasion. In a similar way, Pantry Magic seeks to provide cooking enthusiasts with professional quality cookware, kitchen tools, cookbooks and a whole range of other culinary and kitchen components to create exciting dishes every time.

The only regional chain of specialty kitchenware stores in Asia Pacific, Pantry Magic's range of products are hand-selected by cooking professionals to ensure that they are simple yet durable and effective tools that professionals and home cooks can rely on for years to come. Attention to detail means bakeware is thick and heavy for even heat distribution, pots and pans always have metal handles attached with rivets so they can go from stove to oven, and designs are time-tested. Visit www.pantry-magic.com to learn more.